BLEST. BROKEN. GIVEN.

Taste my Word before I speak —

Praying that the Lord will
continue to bless you
with new mercies and
give you the desires of
your heart.

Mother Mc Coy

2016

BLEST. BROKEN. GIVEN.

"THIS IS MY STORY; THIS IS MY SONG; PRAISING MY SAVIOR, ALL THE DAY LONG."

By

Susie N. McCoy, EdS

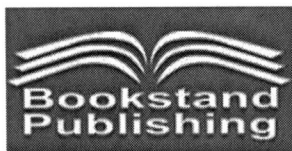

Bookstand Publishing

www.bookstandpublishing.com

Published by
Bookstand Publishing
Morgan Hill, CA 95037
3901_4

ISBN 978-1-61863-528-0

Printed in the United States of America

ACKNOWLEDGEMENTS

This book is dedicated first to my Lord and Savior, Jesus Christ. Philemon 1:6, says, *"That the communication of thy faith may become effectual by the acknowledging of every good thing which is in you in Christ Jesus."* The purpose of this book is to take those God-ordained opportunities and share my faith with others, that I might experience the good things which God has planned for me. In obedience to His Word, to provide freedom and encouragement to the readers of this book, I have communicated my faith by acknowledging my life experiences as I walked humbly with the Lord for over sixty-six years. To God be the Glory!

This book is also dedicated to my family, the Real McCoys. My soul salvation through Jesus Christ ranks the greatest gift that I have ever received. My family is the second greatest gift from God. The Real McCoys include: my late husband of thirty-five years, Bishop Ruel B. McCoy; my oldest son, Bishop M. Ruel McCoy, Sr.; son, Deacon Luke B. McCoy, Sr.; daughters, Dr. Dorcas E. McCoy and Precious A. McCoy; my daughters-in-love, Benona and Elaine; and my grandchildren, Marcus, Jr.; Luke, Jr.; Michael; Lukeeshaa; Markeya, Dondre and Kenshawn. Without God placing these people in my life to encourage, challenge, and correct me, this material would not have been possible. *"Lo, children are and heritage of the Lord: and the fruit of the womb is his reward. As arrows are in the hand of a mighty man; so are children of the youth."*

Special thanks to my spiritual daughter, Suzette Goosby Dixon, a retired educator from the Polk County School System, for her tireless work in editing the memoir while preserving my voice and perspective. Thanks for your support and encouragement throughout this long labor of love.

I am eternally grateful to God for my armor bearers and Spiritual daughters, Carol Moore of New York and Carol Moore of Ohio. Like Aaron and Hur, they held up my hands during my Presidential tenure. I could not have received more love, nor better care than that which they provided. Carol Moore of New York walked beside me every step of the way. She dressed me in the finest. She continues to honor me as her Spiritual Mother and leader. Finally, to the "Whosoevers" who read and are helped by my writing, I dedicate this book to you. Even though this literary work has its limitations, it is my hope that with God's help you will find encouragement, strength, and practical solutions to your problems and challenges. It is my desire to share my faith while offering practical approaches to success.

TABLE OF CONTENTS

GOD'S WILL IS NOT ALWAYS EASY BUT IT'S ALWAYS RIGHT

whatsoever things are just, whatsoever things are pure, whatsoever things are lovely, whatsoever things are of good report; if there be any virtue, and if there be any praise, think on these things."

teach, nor to usurp authority over the man, but to be in silence."

Foreword by Dorcas E. McCoy, PhD

"The aged women likewise, that they be in behavior as becometh holiness...teachers of good things...that they may teach the young women" Titus 2:3-4 (KJV)

Have you ever heard someone deliver an inspiring speech and thought to yourself how much you would like a copy of it in order to insert excerpts of the speech into something you are developing? God has answered your prayers. **Blest. Broken. Given.** is a precious and priceless memoir of an authentically Apostolic Mother openly sharing lessons from her life's journey in order to encourage, enlighten and equip others to live victoriously.

The memoir is a compilation of inspirational writings, public speeches, scholarly papers, fund raising programs for women's groups and churches, lesson outlines, administrative proposals and more. The reader will experience a gamut of emotions as the essence of the title gradually emerges through an intriguing, strategically arranged, assortment of topics. The central theme is that the joy of being **blessed** is not fully realized until one learns to accept the power of God's strength in **brokenness**. Although the pain of brokenness seems personal and individual, it takes the humility, strength, and wisdom acquired through the journey to fully prepare one to be completely **given** to others. Like Christ, our pain leads to others' gain.

God uses the wisdom and unique experiences of the older women to teach, train and temper the younger women. The author's extraordinary ability to relate to and effectively reach younger women and people of diverse backgrounds and levels of preparation is apparent throughout her writings. This innate "Titus Two Teaching Talent" is undoubtedly linked to her passion for education and continuous thirst for knowledge, even as a 75 years young, seasoned senior. Over the course of my professional career spanning across eighteen years of teaching and administration in higher education, I have yet to find a more disciplined student. I have entered her room early in the morning and late nights, intending to check on her while she slept. However, what I often discovered was the aged woman still working. She spends countless hours writing and studying. I often ask if she is preparing to teach the first Sunday Women's Class for our Church's Academy of Excellence, external speaking engagement, or doing homework. Many times, she tells me that she is not sure whom she is preparing to deliver the inspirations of her writing to, but she knows that God has given her something to be given to someone.

We have shared great laughs down through the years by attending conventions and seminars in which upon arrival, she is asked to replace a speaker who did not show or to spontaneously share words of inspiration. She readily fulfills the role with confidence and professionally prepared handouts, which are always amazingly appropriate for the affair. With this copy of **Blest. Broken. Given.** you too can be prepared to rise to any occasion. The author is a pattern of good works, a teacher of good things. I cannot thank my God enough for allowing the DNA of this author to be the foundation of my existence. She is the essence of true Motherhood. Readers will remain glued to the pages as they too experience rich lessons of life from the author's wit, wisdom and willingness to share.   Mother Superior, thank you for your vision to imagine the unimaginable and your courage to reach the unreachable.

Dorcas E. McCoy, PhD
Dorcas E. McCoy, PhD

PREFACE

This book is my first effort to publish and share my life experiences. I started this project at the age of sixty-six and put it down for a while. Now, at the age of seventy-five, I have picked it up again to finally get it finished. During these past nine years, many things have happened which would not have been included if I had completed this labor of love earlier. It is as if the Lord is saying, "Now, you are old enough to tell your story, in love and joy."

In June of 2008, at the age of 70, I graduated salutatorian from the W. L. Bonner Bible College in Columbia, South Carolina, with a BS in Religious Studies and a focus in Women's Ministries. In August of 2011, at the age of 73, I completed the necessary online course work, through Liberty Theological Seminary in Lynchburg, Virginia, for my MA in Theological Studies. At present, I am completing the necessary requirements for an Education Specialist (Ed.S.) in Educational Leadership, at Liberty University. I am now on track to have this degree conferred in August of 2013 when I am 75 years of age.

I would like to share with the Body of Christ the principles, which I have learned. Those precious pearls of wisdom God entrusted to me are reflected in this volume. Writing a personal testimony has been a challenging undertaking for me. However, I am humbled by the task of putting into words those things that I pray will be helpful to others. I have experienced the Grace of God, which allowed me to complete this privileged assignment in spite of my limitations. This book contains stories of how I was bruised but was always delivered. The title, *Blest, Broken, Given*, (Matthew 26:26) means the process necessary to receive the body of Christ.

(God gave me the word **"BLEST"** as one of the words for the title of this book. It is the past tense and past participle of bless. It has the same meaning as blessed).

I can truly say that I was in a war, wounded, with scars, but with God's help and the prayers of others, I was able to rise again, pick up my cross, and follow Jesus with joy and determination. To God be the Glory for the things He has done in my life.

CHAPTER ONE

MY CONVERSION
*"He that believeth and is baptized shall be saved; but
he that believeth not shall be damned."*
Mark 16:16

"They overcame him by the words of their testimony"
is one of my personal mottos. It presents an important
spiritual principle, which showed me the path to spiritual
victory. With this in mind, I am grateful to be able to put
my conversion testimony in writing.

I was converted at the age of nine. I am now
seventy-five years of age, but I can still remember how
and what happened. We were living in Scotch Plains,
New Jersey just three doors down the street from the
Refuge Church of Our Lord Jesus Christ of the Apostolic
Faith, Inc. The church's address was 301 Plainfield
Avenue. Many times the church did not have a Pastor.
Missionaries from New York would come over and
evangelize the neighborhood.

One day, in 1943, a missionary, named Mother Mack
knocked on our door. She was dressed in a long black
dress with a wide white collar and a large brim, flat top
hat. She asked my mother if she would let her children
come to the church to attend Sunday school. My mother
said yes. My oldest sister, Mary, my brother, Charles, Jr.
(we called "Yookie" or Junior) and I, started going to
Sunday school. At that time, my mother only had three
children. I ended up with four sisters and three brothers:
Mary; Charles (Yookie); James Thomas (Jimmy); Etta
Louis (Wendy); Helen Elizabeth (Betsy); Robert; and Eval
(Toni).

Some of the original members of that congregation told me that I was around five years old when they witnessed me experiencing the indwelling of the Holy Spirit. I think I was actually nine years old because that's when I was old enough to believe for myself. Since I have matured, I've accepted the baptism over because I felt that I understood more clearly the scripture that states *"He that underline believeth and is baptized shall be saved."*

I noticed that Mother Mack would come to the church around noon each day to pray, so I started joining her. It was a one-on-one experience when she helped to pray me through in order to accept Christ as my personal Savior. Often I would imitate what I thought the others doing when they were singing, only to learn when I could read out of a song book, that I was actually singing the wrong words. Sometimes, even now, I rejoice within when I recite the words that I learned as a child.

My testimony is that the Lord is able to keep the young if you desire to be kept. In my day "holiness" was really strict. I wasn't allowed to go out and run around and play with the other children. I didn't even participate in gym class when I attended high school because I didn't wear shorts. I took a course in health in order to get the necessary credit for graduation. No Prom- no dancing (worldly music) -no movies (sitting in the seat of the scornful), etc. I wasn't even allowed to date. I remained pure. I only saw my husband five times before we were married. We married in 1959 and my husband died in 1993; two months short of 35 years (until death did we part).

I've no regrets through it all! I realized that the Lord had a calling on my life from the beginning. The Lord allowed me to hold the highest position a female can have in my church denomination. I was elected President of the International Women's Council, which includes approximately 30,000 females in the United States and 10 different countries. I was blessed to hear the Chief Apostle of the organization say, "Out of all the females that sat in this seat, Mother McCoy came closest to being an Apostolic Mother." Now, I am waiting for that more important statement from the Almighty One: "Well done thou good and faithful servant!"

Mary, Susie, Yookie, Wendy, Bet, Robert, Jimmy and Toni

4

CHAPTER TWO

A TRIBUTE TO MY SPIRITUAL MOTHER
ON HER 99th BIRTHDAY

MOTHER ANNIE ROBINSON GRAYER

"*Render therefore to all their due; custom to whom custom; fear to whom fear; honour to whom honour.*"
Romans 13:7

"Lo, children are and heritage of the LORD: and the fruit of the womb is his reward. As arrows are in the hand of a mighty man; so are children of thy youth."

The following is what I recall as my mind of 75 years reflects:

It was October 18, 1943 or 1945 when a young couple came to pastor us at the Refuge Church of Our Lord Jesus Christ, Scotch Plains, New Jersey. Mother Grayer was in her early thirties; her husband was thirteen or fifteen years older. That was when Elder and Mother Robert S. Grayer and their children: Evelyn, Shirley, Robert Jr., George, Joan, and Inez became our first family. The oldest daughter Esther and her son, Alex did not come. Their youngest children, Dorothy and Michael, were born later.

They made weekly trips from Trenton, New Jersey to Scotch Plains, which was 46 miles, one way Our Sunday school started at 2 p.m., which allowed Elder and Mother Grayer sufficient time to arrive before 11:00 a.m. Morning worship. They made this drive many years before moving to Somerville, New Jersey.

5

On the way from Trenton, they would stop in Princeton and pick-up the Bracey family. His musician, Sister Louise, who eventually married Deacon Bob, became Sister Louise Johnson. The family included Sister Louise, her brother Paul, her sister and their Mother. (Another Sister Muriel started in the latter years). Paul played the harmonica. This family was gifted musically and contributed greatly to the service.

I, Susie Nelson, was the first young person saved under this ministry. I remember being baptized during the winter in a trough down stairs in the kitchen area. The water was extremely cold. Mothers Mack, Brooks, and Wade, missionaries from New York, came over and evangelized the area surrounding the church. The two Ford brothers and Elder Campbell came to shepherd us; but they did not stay. Mother Lillian Ford of Red Banks, New Jersey was our State Missionary President. We had 13 churches throughout the state and a female started them all.

I remember Mother Grayer as our ABYPU President. She gave the challenge for all the youth to memorize the 12th Chapter of Ecclesiastes. I was the ONLY one who completed this assignment. She awarded me the first, second, and third prize. What a woman of wisdom! That lesson helped formed my life expectation because I remembered the Lord in my youth; now I can enjoy my senior years all the more. To God be the Glory! Thank you, Mother Grayer.

Mother Grayer gave me advice that has stayed with me and helped through the years. One was: "Don't wear your feelings on your sleeves. If you do and a scab covers the wound, someone will rub the scab off and you will always be bleeding." Thank you, Mother Grayer.

I have tried to imitate her lifestyle so much. For example, I met a man that had been married before. He was 10 years older than I and lived in New Smyrna Beach, Florida. His church was located in Sorrento, Florida and was 46 miles from his home. I saw that as a sign that I was to marry him, so I could be like Mother Grayer. Thank you, Mother Grayer.

During the early years of my marriage, we would meet every June in Southern Pines, North Carolina. Mother Grayer and I would spend time having our "mother to daughter chats." She instructed me how to develop into a woman among women. Thank you, Mother Grayer!

Once Mother Grayer told me that after I married and moved to Florida, people would ask, "How is your daughter in Florida?" She would give them an answer and not try to explain that I was not her biological daughter. Thank you, Mother Grayer!

I was told that Philippians 4:8 was Bishop Grayer's favorite Scripture and to always include it on the anniversary program cover. Every Sunday morning worship service started with the singing of, "All Hail the Power of Jesus Name" or "Holy, Holy, Holy." We learned to sing hymns and all the verses. No drums or tambourines were played during the morning worship service. There was an evangelistic type service at night with stirring "testimonies." Thank you, Mother Grayer for that sound foundation to build on.

We stayed in church all day, every Sunday, starting with the 11 o'clock service. I can still see the choir marching down the aisle in blue robes, singing "We are Marching to Zion." Sister Julia Quarrels sat on the front row, and Sister Amy Parrott sat in the middle. Our main leader was Sister Evelyn Counts. The altos were; Sister

Carrie Nelson, Sister Dorothy Kirkwood, Mary Jackson and Sister Virginia Morrow (Jenkins). Brother Paul Bracey was the tenor and Brother Alfred Quarrels, Sr. was the baritone. Thank you, Mother Grayer.

In the later years, we moved Sunday school from the afternoon to the morning. That may have been when the Grayers moved to Scotch Plains. I was in Sunday School Class #1 and my teacher was Mother Grayer's daughter, Evelyn. She taught from a chart hanging on the wall, which had a picture larger than the one on the cards that we took home. I was taught the Scripture and the ways of the Lord during my youth. Thank you, Mother Grayer!

On Sunday, we usually brought a packed lunch basket from home or we could purchase something to eat which a different auxiliary provided each Sunday. The Grayer family always ate free. We had a 3 o'clock afternoon service, the ABYPU was held at 6 o'clock and night service started at 7 o'clock. Thank you, Mother Grayer!

You taught me how to prepare my Sunday meals as I cooked breakfast in order to save time. We had homemade ice cream, with Sister Ethel winding the crank, pouring rock salt and we would wait to lick the dasher. What about Sister Irene's three layer coconut cake? Does anyone remember my Godmother, Mother Frieda Johnson's, jelly rolls and yeast rolls? You must remember Sister Hattie Stewart's pound cakes! We were taught how to cut the cake into fours, and then each section was cut into three slices. There were only twelve slices per cake. Mother Grayer taught us that we would sin, if we charged people for an insufficient amount of food. Thank you, Mother Grayer!

You reached out to the blind. I vividly remember Sister Bryant and how she sometimes stayed with you. I recall

8

how your family often picked her up and brought her to church. I can only remember one "friend girl" Sister Alberta Collins Long, who was your friend before you married. I do not remember ever seeing you in the driver's seat of an automobile in your marriage. I can still recall sitting and waiting without complaints with you as Elder Grayer took different saints home after church. You remained kind and generous. Your home would be the place for visiting evangelists and missionaries to stay. This was a great help to me as my own husband's ministry grew.

When we traveled throughout the state of New Jersey, we always followed our leader with a motorcade of cars. Sometimes we did not even know the address; we just followed leadership. One story circulated (and I believe it is true) that someone followed a person into their driveway, thinking that they were following Bishop Grayer.

On August 8, 1959, fifty-four years ago, I got married and left the Scotch Plains Church of Our Lord Jesus Christ. I do not know anything about the Refuge Church of Christ in Plainfield and I have never seen or dreamed about you being there. I remember you from Scotch Plains and am grateful to God for the many memories of the time we spent together there with you as my Spiritual Mother. Thank You, Mother Grayer!

Precious memories, how they linger,
How the every flood my soul,
In the stillness of the midnight,
Precious sacred scenes unfold.

Precious memories,
unseen angels Sent from somewhere
to my soul
How they linger ever near me And the
sacred past unfold.

Precious father, loving Mother Grayer
Fly across the lonely years
And old home scenes of my childhood In
fond memory appear.

In the stillness of the midnight Echoes from
the past I hear
Old time singing, gladness bringing From
that lovely land somewhere

As I travel on life's pathway
Know not what the years may hold As I
ponder, hope grows fonder
Precious memories flood my soul.

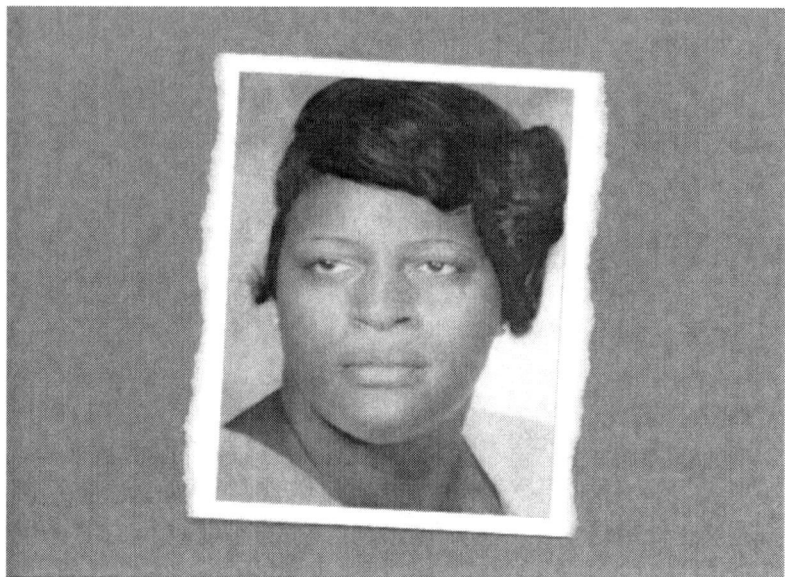

CHAPTER THREE

MY PERSONAL PHILOSOPHY OF WORSHIP

*"Give unto the Lord the glory due unto his name;
worship the Lord in the beauty of holiness."* Psalm 29:2

Introduction

Using Scriptural principles and content analysis, this research will highlight the varied philosophical perspectives of my personal philosophy of worship. Realizing that philosophy is the *"why"* and the *"how"* of a topic and worship is *the biblical response to God, resulting from an understanding of biblical truth about God.* This paper will provide the opportunity for me to clearly articulate and present the results of my investigation on my philosophy of worship. The experience of gathering, interpreting, documenting information, developing and organizing my ideas, and conclusions, and communicating them clearly have proven to be an important and satisfying part of my education. This research will logically provide biblical, theological, historical, and methodological criteria for my philosophy of worship.

Personal Philosophy of Worship Mission Statement

I will glorify God and make Him known by unashamedly proclaiming the truth of His Word.

Body

As a believer, every decision I make should have a Scriptural, theological basis as its foundation. The Word of God is the only certain, objective source of criteria for decision making. A theology of a topic is what the Bible teaches about that topic. This may be explicit instruction or implicit principles. From that theology must flow a believer's philosophy. Based on the Scriptural principles that have been gathered concerning a topic, the believer must develop a philosophy. It is therefore very important that I develop a sound, Biblical definition of what it means to worship. In reality, worship is why I exist. Any definition that I contrive is insufficient unless it finds its basis in the Word of God.

> John 4:23 (KJV*) "But the hour cometh and now is, when the true worshippers shall worship the Father in spirit and in truth: for the Father seeketh such to worship him."*

Worship is a reverent devotion and allegiance pledge to God; the rituals or ceremonies by which this reverence is expressed. The English word *"worship"* comes from the Old English word *"worthship"* a word that denotes the worthiness of the one receiving the special honor or devotion (*Worship Old & New*).

Throughout Scripture, two elements predominantly characterize worship: *a presentation of truth* and a *response to that truth.* The following are two passages of Scripture which demonstrate this point:

> **Nehemiah 8:1-6** *"So on the first day of the seventh month Ezra the priest brought the Law before the assembly. He read it aloud from daybreak till noon. And all the people listened attentively to the Book of the Law. Ezra praised the Lord, the great God; and all the people lifted their hands and responded, "Amen! Amen! Then they bowed down and **worshiped** the Lord with their faces to the ground."*

> **Matthew 28:9** *"Suddenly Jesus met them. "Greetings,"*

He said. They came to Him, (worshiped Him. "

As noted in these two Scriptur worship involves *a response*, either *a presentation of truth* about God. ' true, Biblical worship: *response to truth.* Jesus summarized this fact when He said in John 4:24 (KJV) "God is a Spirit: and they that *worship* Him must *worship* Him in Spirit (internal response) and in truth" (*Putting an End to Worship Wars*).

My **personal philosophy of worship** is that true worship is not confined to a specific time, like on Sunday morning. All of life should worship God. Every act, thought, and attitude of a believer should be *a response to truth* about God. This is expressed throughout the New Testament, as recorded in Romans 12:1 (KJV*) "I beseech you therefore, brethren, by the mercies of God, that ye present your bodies a living sacrifice, holy, acceptable unto God, which is your reasonable service." (This is your spiritual act of worship).*

There are, three definite biblical worship *"styles"* taught in Scripture. The first one is **Lifestyle of worship,** which is illustrated in Romans 12:1: All of life should be worship. The second type is **Private worship,** which is a more narrowed style of worship. This is when a believer spends dedicated personal time with the Lord in His Word and in prayer. As a believer studies the Word of God, the Holy Spirit will reveal to that person the significance of the Scripture to his or her life. The believer should respond accordingly.

The third style of worship is **congregational worship.** This is the gathering of the people of God in order to corporately worship Him as His people. This form of ip is clearly commanded and exemplified in pture: Psalm 149:1 *"Praise ye the Lord, Sing unto the Lord a new song, and his praise in the congregation of saints."*

Congregational worship was also exemplified in the early Church (Acts 2: 42-47; 13:1-3). It is clear both from Old Testament command and from New Testament examples that God desires believers to lift His praises together. He wants His children to gather for the purpose of honoring Him. This worship is still an individual, heartfelt response toward God, but it is done publicly in the presence of other believers. This brings God even more glory than if it were done privately. C.H. Spurgeon said, "Personal praise is sweet unto God, but congregational praise has a multiplicity of sweetness in it" (What Happened to Worship? A Call to True Worship).

It is also important to recognize the worship language that Paul uses to describe the New Testament Church:

1 Corinthians 3:16-17 (KJV) *"Know ye not that ye are the temple of God, and that the Spirit of God dwelleth in you? If any man defile the temple of God, him shall God destroy; for the temple of God is holy, which temple ye are."*

1 Peter 2:5 (KJV) *"Ye also, as lively stones, are built up a spiritual house, a holy priesthood, to offer up spiritual sacrifices, acceptable to God by Jesus Christ."*

Therefore, congregational worship could be defined as follows:

Congregational worship is a unified chorus of Biblical responses toward God expressed publicly to God resulting from an understanding of Biblical truth about God (The Great Worship Awakening).

From this theology, I determined that my personal philosophy of worship is that worship must first be **God-oriented.** Because worship is specifically designed to be *a response* to God because of Biblical *truth* about Him, God must be the center of the service. Because the Bible is our only objective source of *truth* about God, Scriptural truth about God should be the content of my worship. Because worship is intended to be *a response* to God, therefore, my worship should be directed to God.

Second, my worship must be **doctrine-oriented.** Because as a believer I can respond only when I can understand biblical truth, my worship should be filled with doctrinal truth. Because worship requires understanding doctrine, and understanding doctrine requires work, believers should not shy away from elements in the service that have deep, thought-provoking content.

Third, my worship must be **affection-oriented.** Service elements that excite the passions are not acceptable for worship. "Passions" are emotions that are immediately gratifying, are shallow, and result from emotionalism that by passes the intellect. Since understand of truth is by passed, this kind of emotionalism is not acceptable for my worship. Service elements that develop God-honoring affections should be used for worship. "Affections" are emotion that results from volitional acknowledgment of objective truth. They take work to develop and are more lasting and pleasing to the Lord. Affection toward God is the essence of true worship.

Fourth, my worship must be **congregation-oriented.** Because the purpose of my worship is that believers join together as the Body of Christ to express a unified response to God, service elements that are very individualistic or personal do not have a place in congregational worship. Music used in congregational worship should be limited to songs that express objective truth that applies to all Christians.

We have said that true worship has two parts: *a presentation of truth* and *a response to that truth.* Both of these must be present in a worship service for worship to take place. Therefore, every element in the service will facilitate one or both of these.

I believe that God wants us to worship Him by joyous singing of psalms, hymns and spiritual songs, offering Him prayer with thanksgiving, reading and preaching of His Word and the administration of the Sacraments. The people of God should offer Him praise, worship and thanksgiving as required in His Word. To emphasize exegetical, expository preaching, my goal is always to understand what God said, and what He wants me to do as a result.

The following are the scriptures that helped me to form my philosophy of worship:

I believe worship should be:

1. **God-centered:** Celebrating the distinctive roles and work of the Trinity
   a. God the Father (Ephesians 1:3-6)
   b. God the Son (Ephesians 1:7-12
   c. God the Holy Spirit (Ephesians 1:13-14)

2. **Bible-based:** Concentrating on teaching the truth of God's Word
   a. Pray the Word (1 Timothy 2:1)
   b. Read the Word (1 Timothy 4:13)
   c. Sing the Word (Colossians 3:16; Ephesians 5:19)
   d. Preach the Word (2 Timothy 4:2)

3. **Gospel-declaring:** Communicating the good news of Jesus Christ
    a. Man's sin (Romans 3:23)
    b. Sin's consequences (Romans 6:23)
    c. God's solution (John 3:16)
    d. Christ's sacrifice (Romans 5:8)
    e. Man's faith (Ephesians 2:8-9
    f. God's gift (Romans 6:23)

4. **Church-building:** Cultivating the common good of the Church
    a. Edify the body (Ephesians 2:19-22; 1 Cor. 14:26)
    b. Educating the believer (Colossians 3:16)
    c. Engaging the head and heart
    d. Encouraging unity (Romans 15:5-6)
    e. Evangelizing the lost (Matthew 28:18-20)
    f. Exhorting saint and sinner I value corporate worship that is:

5. **Congregational** (Psalm 111:1; 149:1)

I believe that our chief instrument of praise is our voices. This impacts our choices of music and instrumentation. During congregational singing, the congregation's voice should be primary. Instrumentation and corporate worship leaders should enhance the congregation's voice, not cover it up. I believe that the congregation should have an active role in corporate worship services through attitude, action, thought, preparation, and response. Corporate worship is not passive entertainment, but intentional engagement. I come to church ready to participate by paying attention and involving myself in the worship in order to bear witness to the message being declared.

6. **Excellent** (Psalm 33:1-3)

I believe that worship should be intentionally planned, creatively designed, adequately rehearsed, skillfully led, and intentional evaluated in order to better promote an atmosphere of worship.

7. **Appropriate and Relevant**

I believe that worship should be both, appropriate in holding exclusively to God's commands in Scripture as our rule of worship, and relevant in applying those commandments in legitimate, and often nontraditional ways. Although our worship is directed to God, our songs should be understandable and usable by the congregation.

8. **Authentic and Genuine** (Isaiah 29:13; Matthew 15:8-9)

I believe that worship should be done in a sincere and humble manner. Vain repetitions and empty exercise have no place in heartfelt worship.

9. **Trans-generational** (Philippians 2:1-7; Romans 15:5-7)

I believe that worship should transcend generational barriers by recognizing and embracing an appreciation for various worship styles, tunes and texts. I believe in forging a form of corporate worship within a framework of Biblical theology that takes seriously both our history and our contemporary reality. The primary characteristic of my worship will be that it is based upon the truth of God's Word. Scripture alone takes precedence over opinion, tradition and preference. I believe that worship should unite the church, not divide it.

My philosophy of worship is to value a public worship form that communicates the supremacy of God in my life and it will focus on God. The form may vary from week to week as long as God continues to meet me in worship. I will encourage an expectancy and eagerness to draw near to God in reviving and renewing power.

My personal philosophy of worship is that one must be fervent, Biblical, Spirit anointed, God-exalting, personally helpful preaching; one that will pray that God's Word continues to run and be glorified among us as greatly in the future as it has in the past, as all aspects of worship are shaped and permeated by the Word of God.

Because I value the importance of old and new, historic and current, my philosophy of worship is to pray that "the Holy Spirit may lead me into ways of worship that are continuous with the historic witness of worship given to the church throughout its history in the world, and at the same time He may lead us into the discovery of new forms and patterns that meet the needs of the people of our day" (R. Webber, "Worship Old and New"). I will continue to be a "both/and" person who cherishes all the richness and freshness that comes from God.

Because my philosophy of worship is to know the importance of both head and heart in the worship experience, I will continue to fill my mind with Biblical thinking about God, others, myself, and life, while at the same time putting renewed and greater emphasis on giving expression to my heart's affections for God during worship.

Because my philosophy of worship is that one must go hard after God as all satisfying end in Himself, I will increasingly plan the worship service for greater opportunities to linger in the presence of the Lord. He is the treasure, the pearl of great price, and I will come with an earnestness and wholeheartedness on my past that desires God more than anything.

Because I value authenticity and transparency in communicating in large and small group settings, I will strive for genuineness when in groups or by myself. Whether rehearsed or spontaneous, I will strive to be real before God and others.

Because I value vulnerability with my imperfections that encourage candor, not concealment, I will minister in the strength that God supplies as I am sustained by His grace, acknowledging that my treasure is in jars of clay to show that this all-surpassing power is not my own.

Conclusion

The church has had centuries of battles. It has fought theological battles and those who lost were martyred; such as Servetus who was burned at the stake by John Calvin. It's had turf wars when denominations fourth over the right to evangelize the islands of the South Seas. There have always been conquest wars such as The Crusades in their capture of Jerusalem. The Church has had "blood and guts" battles such as the one in 1531, where Ulrich Zwingli, the Christian patriot died defending the Bible against tradition. The church has fought over doctrine, policy, wicked leaders, and corruption, appointing people to positions and even over the battles of statues in churches. Today's most agonizing battles are over worship!!

The first murder grew out of an angry fight between two brothers who disagreed over worship. Was a vegetable worship of God better than a blood sacrifice? While the first disagreement involved a substance question, today's disagreement is over methodology, i.e. how we worship.

Since worship is the most powerful force exerted by a creature, then it is only natural that it is going to be one of the most difficult energies to harness and direct. Like the enormous danger of atomic nuclear energy, let's pray that worship can be directed for the good of mankind, not its destruction.

That's why it is important that everyone have their own personal philosophy of worship, to be able to follow their own heart as it follows the Word of God. Worship is a face-to-face encounter with the living God based on a regeneration experience, prompted by the Holy Spirit, and resulting in the exaltation of God's Glory. Simply speaking, worship is giving the *worth ship* to God that He deserves, because He is God. Therefore, worship should be an emotional, intellectual, and volitional response to God. Because of the relationship between worshipper and God who is worshipped, worship is a growing thing and a dynamic entity. ***Worship is personal, and true worship cannot be divorced from the worshipper.*** Worship, is an earnest effort to re- create the conditions and experiences that have been found to deepen a person's relationship with God.

Worship involves the intellectual process, but it is more than mere knowledge of God. Worship stirs the emotions, but is more than the expression of passion. ***Worship comes from a person's choice to surrender his/her will to God, but is more than a mere decision.*** The heart is moved by biblical facts to recreate the fundamental human experiences of praise, adoration and exaltation of God for who He is and what He has done specifically worshipper.

Bibliography

Giglio, Louie. *The Air I Breathe.* Multnomah Books, 2006

Hall, Christopher. *Learning Theology with the Church Fathers.* Downers Grove, IL: IV, 2002 Hargreeves, Sam & Sara. *How Would Jesus Lead Worship.* Bible Reading Fellowship, 2009 Hughes, Tim. *Holding Nothing Back.* Christianbook.com, 2007

Kauflin, Bob. *Worship Matters.* Crossway Books, 2008

Liesch, Barry. *People In the Presence of God.* Zondervan, 1988

Litfin, Bryan M. *Getting to Know the Church Fathers: An Evangelical Introduction:*

Grand Rapid, Brazos, 2007

Mark, Robin. *Warrior Poets.* Ambassador International, 2007 Park, Andy. *To Know More.* InterVarsity, 2002

Piper, John. *Desiring God.* Multnomah, 2003

Redman, Matt. *The Unquenchable Worshipper.* Regal, 2001 *Facedown.* Regal, 2004

Redman, Robert. *The Great Worship Awakening.* San Francisco, CA. Jossey-Bass, 2002

Smither, Edward. *Augustine as Mentor: A Model for Preparing Spiritual Leaders.*

Nashville, TN: B & H Academic, 2009

Sorge, Bob. *Exploring Worship: A Practical Guide to Praise and Worship.* Oasis House, 1987 Towns, Elmer. *Putting an End to Worship Wars.* Nashville. Broadman & Holman, 1997

The Ten Greatest Revivals Ever. Virginia Beach. Academix 2005

Tozer, A. W. *What Happen to Worship? A Call to True Worship.* Christian Publications 1985

Webber, Robert. *Worship Old & New.* Grand Rapids. Zondervan, 1994

Music and Arts in Christian Worship. Nashville. Star Song, 1994

75TH BIRTHDAY & GRADUATION CELEBRATION

Mother Susie

LPGA INTERNATIONAL CLUB HOUSE
1000 CHAMPIONS DRIVE
DAYTONA BEACH, FL 32124

TIME:
6:00 P.M.

ATTIRE:
ALL WHITE, DRESSY CASUAL

TICKETS: $50

RSVP:
WWW. THEMOTHERSUPERIOR.

CHAPTER FOUR

A PRAYER FOR MY LEADERS

Lord Jesus Christ, I love and adore you. I magnify your Holy Name. Apostle Paul has made it quite clear, in your word, that in order for me to lead a quiet and peaceful life in all godliness and honesty; I am to pray for all men, but especially for those who are in authority.

He wrote in 1 Timothy 2:1-4 *"I exhort therefore, that, first of all, supplication, prayers, intercession, and giving of thanks, be make for all men; For kings, and for all that are in authority; that we may lead a quiet and peaceable life in all godliness and honesty. For this is good and acceptable in the sight of God our Savior; who will have all men to be saved, and to come, unto the knowledge of the truth."*

Lord Jesus, I come before you in faith, praying for ALL of humankind (male and female) that are in authority, those that are Christian and for those who do not claim you as their personal Savior. Your Word beseeched, urged me to pray for "Kings" our national rulers and for "all that are in authority" like the church leader of COOLJC because my very happiness and success depends to a very large extent on these people.

Lord, I humbly pray for Chief Apostle W.L. Bonner, Apostle Gentle L. Groover, Sr., Apostle Matthew Norwood, Bishop James B. Darby, Bishop M. Ruel McCoy, Sr., the Apostle's Board, the Bishop's Board, the Presbyter's Board, the International Union of Deacons, the Women's Auxiliary Leaders, the Youth Auxiliary Leaders and leaders everywhere, both within and outside of the Church of our Lord Jesus Christ of the Apostolic, Faith, Inc.

According to your Word in supplication and humility, I pray that each leader will love God with all their heart, soul, mind, and strength. I pray that the Holy Spirit will work in a mighty way in the heart of each leader and that they will follow biblical principles in making daily decision as they attempt to live righteously.

I pray that these leaders will live in **harmony with YOUR WILL,** with other leaders, and with the people they lead as they exhibit a Christ like attitude towards one another. For those who do not know You, I pray for their salvation. I am interceding for the marriage of each of our leaders. I pray that each leader will work hard to have a Godly marriage that can be shown as an example to others. I pray that each leader will gently cherish their spouse and that there will be a biblical understanding between the two parties regarding their individual roles in the marriage.

I offer up this prayer of **thanksgiving** for each leader. I thank you Lord for placing them in my life. I pray that my leaders will have an alert and thankful heart. I pray that they will have YOUR love in their hearts for the people they are leading. I pray that they will have knowledge, wisdom, and understanding of YOUR WILL for their lives. I pray that they will have a complete understanding of who You are and how to develop a relationship with YOU!

Lord, you said in your Word that if I asked anything in your name without doubt that you would grant the request. I beseech you in your precious Son's Name, Lord Jesus Christ, to bless our leaders. As you have done for me, I am asking you to heal any hurts the leaders have suffered due to their leadership roles. I am praying that the leaders will serve the Lord with gladness and encourage those that they lead to live Christ-honoring lives. In Jesus' Name. **AMEN.**

A TRIBUTE TO MY DECEASED BROTHER IN CHRIST

"Finally, brethren, whatsoever things are true, whatsoever things are honest, whatsoever things are just, whatsoever things are pure, whatsoever things are lovely, whatsoever things are of good report; if there be any virtue, and if there be any praise, think on these things." **Philippians 4:8**

"For me to live is Christ, and to die is gain," said the Apostle Paul. We know that this would be Bishop Jenkins' message if he were able to give us a message from Paradise; where he has gone to be with the Lord.

To his Thessalonian friends Paul wrote, *"I would not have you to be ignorant, brethren, concerning them which are asleep, that ye sorrow not, even as others which have no hope"* (I Thessalonians 4:13). Hope of what? What possible HOPE can bring comfort at such a time as this, when we mourn the passing of our leader?

"For if we believe that Jesus died and rose again, even so them also which sleep in Jesus will God bring with him" (I Thessalonians 4:14). *"Wherefore comfort one another with these words"* (I Thessalonians 4:18).

As far as we have any knowledge, man is the only one of God's created beings, which God has given the information that all earthly life must end in death. The experience and observations of mankind early in life, impresses upon man's mind the fact, that death is the common lot of all. *"Precious in the sight of the Lord is the death of the saints"* (Psalm 116:15). We have the promises of God that death, which men most fear, shall be to us the most blessed of experiences dependent only upon our perfect trust in Him.

For whether we live, we live unto the Lord; and whether we die, we die unto the Lord; whether we live therefore, or die, we belong to the Lord.

Therefore, my brother in Christ made preparation and on Sunday morning, April 18, 2010, at 10:10 he made the transition. *"Blessed be the God and Father of our Lord Jesus Christ, which according to His abundant mercy hath begotten us again unto a lively hope by the resurrection of Jesus Christ from the dead, to an inheritance incorruptible, and undefiled, and that fadeth not away, reserved in Heaven for us, who are kept by the power of God through faith unto salvation ready to be revealed in the last time"* (I Peter 1:3-5).

"There remaineth therefore a rest to the people of God" (Hebrews 4:9). For over fifty years, my brother in Christ worked long and faithfully throughout the State of Florida. He carried the Great Commission found in Matthew 28:18-20 with the Greatest Commandment found in Matthew 22:37-38. So let us praise God that Bishop Jenkins has found a place of rest in God. Let the family of my brother in Christ be comforted, for our loved one is only sleeping, and will awake in a land of rest.

He was a strong, hard worker, who did everything with all of his might. When he sang (even if the words were wrong), he would open his mouth so wide that if you looked you could see his tonsils. Such steady grind and constant work wore down his body. His physical strength weakened, and affliction fell upon him. He was tired and weary. So, he took his bed in October of 2009, often in pain and misery, and patiently waited, happily and good natured on the orders from the Lord. He devotedly served until (his) last Sunday when his spirit-filled soul took its flight across death's stream. At this moment he rests from his labor. I was told that one of his last requests to his family was, *"Help, me up so that I can praise the Lord with Bishop Ross and Bishop McCoy."*

We must not mourn for our brother in Christ as those without hope; for he has gone to get the great reward promised to all who faithfully serve our Lord and Savior Jesus Christ.

"...Blessed are the dead who die in the Lord..." (Revelation 14:13). I rejoice that, in the midst of grief, I am assured that his passing has brought him eternal joy and fellowship with God. He has received the Crown of Righteousness which is laid up for all the faithful. He was dependable, sincere, devoted to the work of the Lord and was genuine in all of his doings.

I call him my brother in Christ because my family affectionately called him *"Uncle C. J."* In the lives of the McCoys, he did all that an uncle could or would do just as if we were biologically related. We weren't. However, we are blood related through the purging and shedding of the precious Blood of our Lord and Savior, Jesus Christ.

Don't think of him as gone away
His journey has just begun
Life holds many facets The Earth is only one

Just think of him as resting From the sorrows and
the tears In a place of warmth and comfort
Where there are no days and years

Think how he must be wishing
That we could know today How nothing but our

sadness Can really pass away
And think of him as living

In the hearts of those he touched For nothing loved
is ever lost And he was loved so much.

*"And God shall wipe away all tears from their eyes; and
there shall be no more death, neither sorrow, nor crying,
neither shall there be any more pain..."* (Revelation 21:4).
*"Peace I leave with you, my peace I give unto you: not as
the world giveth, give I unto you. Let not your heart be
troubled; neither let it be afraid"* (John 14:27).

Cheif Apostle W. L. Bonner

L-R Top: Apostle M. Norwood, Apostle G. Groover, Bishop J. Darby
Bottom: Bishop C. Jenkins, Bishop M. Ruel McCoy, Sr. Minister M. McCoy, Jr.

CHAPTER FIVE

SUBJECT: WAITING FOR THESE THREE "Ps"– PROMISE-POWER -PENTECOST

*"And, being assembled together with them, that they should not depart from Jerusalem, but wait for the **promise** of the Father, which saith he, ye have heard of me." "But ye shall receive **power**, after that the Holy Ghost is come upon you..." "And when the day of **Pentecost** was fully come, they were all with one accord in one place."*

Acts 1:4-8 (Read together Aloud)

PRAY

INTRODUCTION: In this text, forty days after the Resurrection, Jesus is giving His followers strict instructions to go and wait for the *promise* of the Father, to receive *power* on the Day of *Pentecost.*

When the disciples asked about the timing of the Kingdom, Jesus let them know that they were concerned about the wrong thing. They (we) needed to keep the main thing the main thing. Our Lord knew that His ascension and the teaching of the Holy Spirit would soon end these expectations, and therefore only gave them a rebuke.

What they needed was to wait to receive power. They needed power of the Holy Spirit coming upon them. They needed the baptism of the Holy Spirit, and so do we. They needed this power to be a witness, and so do we.

The Master told them that they should not depart from Jerusalem, but wait for the promise of the Father. The Holy Spirit was involved in the creation and has been involved in every generation of mankind since; but Pentecost brought something totally new involving the Holy Spirit. Let us notice the three "P's" in the text:

THE PROMISE. "But ye shall receive power, after that the Holy Ghost is come upon you." The believers can claim this promise.

1. The promise of power is given and within it is the thought of authority or dynamic works

2. In obedience to the Master's command the early believers is to wait patiently, prayerfully and purposefully; Luke 24:29.

3. The obedience of the early believers was not in vain; Acts 2:1-4; 4:8-10.

4. The Holy Spirit indwells in every believer today, to produce mighty works; John 14:17; Acts 8:29; 10:19, 20.

When Jesus was baptized, the Holy Spirit descended upon Him and stayed throughout His earthly life. When He was about to die on the cross, the Holy Spirit left Him. When Jesus gave His followers strict instruction to go and wait. No one could ever have even imagined the changes that would come into their lives by waiting for the three P's, the Promise, Power and Pentecost.

THE POWER AND THE PURPOSE: He has given us power for a purpose, to be a witness for Him.

1. At Pentecost , power was received to witness by life and by lips; 2 Cor. 3:2; Acts 8:4.

2. At Pentecost, power was received to testify courageously; Acts 4:21.

3. At Pentecost, power was received to live victoriously; Romans 6:14.

4. At Pentecost, power was received to live fervently; Romans 5:5.

5. At Pentecost, power was received to pray effectively; Acts 12:5-19.

6. At Pentecost, power was received to cause individual to give in a generous way; I Corinthians 16:2.

AT PENTECOST THE HOLY SPIRIT WAS GIVEN A NEW TEMPLE IN WHICH TO DWELL.

- The Holy Spirit indwelt the tabernacle Moses constructed. (Exodus 40:34)

- Solomon later built a permanent temple in which the Holy Spirit indwelt (I Kings 8:10-11).

- On the Day of Pentecost, the Holy Spirit came to indwell in the believers; which is the Church (I Peter 2:5).

One hundred twenty followers of Jesus gathered in an upper room and waited. When the Holy Spirit came, everyone was filled, indwelt and so it has been every since that hour. Every believer in Jesus is immediately indwelt by the Holy Spirit. When God enters a place, everyone is made aware of His presence. It is as marvelous, powerful and memorable as it was in that upper room with the sound of a might wind, tongues like fire and speaking in other unlearned languages.

The Holy Spirit came to each INDIVIDUAL believer at Pentecost. Jesus promised that each one would be a temple and that every born again child of God would be individual indwelt (John 14:17; I Corinthians 6:19).

It was different in the Old Testament, for the Holy Spirit never indwelt everyone. When it did, it was only for a specific length of time and purpose (Numbers 11:15).

- For Moses to lead the people out of Egypt.

- For the people to have the skills to make Aaron's priestly garments and to make the tabernacle according to God's Divine Plan. (Exodus 31:1-11)

- The Holy Spirit came upon Gideon, upon Daniel and others as well.

Jesus spoke of the high privilege that those who believed in Him would have (Matthew 11:11). Jesus said that there was no man greater than John the Baptist; yet the Holy Spirit never indwelt him as he lived under the Old Testament guidelines. Today's believers have greater opportunities and privileges than even John the Baptist. Many of the prophets died without receiving the promise, but God have provided greater things for us that they without us cannot be made perfect.

SINCE PENTECOST, THE HOLY SPIRIT HAS NEVER BEEN WITHDRAWN FROM THE BELIEVER.

Today we are in the age of Grace and there is no possibility of the Holy Spirit departing from the believer. Once a person is saved, the Holy Spirit indwells that person forever and gives that person a personal gift to be used for the Lord (John 14:16). However the person can lose fellowship with Him.

Paul reminded the weak and sinful Corinthians that we may grieve, hurt, quench, buffet, refuse to listen, reject advice, but the Holy Spirit will never be withdrawn from us. Even though a person is a fruitless, poor child, the Holy Spirit will live within the believer forever. **IF** ever a child of God, **ALWAYS** a child of God.

CONCLUSION:

ONE MIGHT ASK THE QUESTION – WHERE, HOW, WHY and WHAT SHOULD I DO WHILE WAITING?

The Lord said: "Ye shall be witness unto Me both in Jerusalem, and in Judaea, in Samaria, and unto the uttermost part of the earth."

- Jesus said, "The field is the world…." Matthew 13:38

- Jesus said, "… Go ye into the world," Mark 16:15

- The Apostle John said, "….the whole world lieth in wickedness." I John 5:19

- This revolting world ruined by sin needs our witness. Only Christ can deliver it.

Thank God for the 3 P's – the Promise and the Power of Pentecost. How different since the day of Pentecost. Just think, with all our weaknesses, the Holy Spirit is never taken away from us who believe.

Remember Peter? How often did he fall, fail, make mistakes, and go astray? Was the Holy Spirit ever taken from Peter? Jesus even told Peter that Satan was going to sift him again and again and that Peter would fail again and again, but the Holy Spirit never left him. Peter is an example of *persistence, preaching, repentance, exhortation, devotion* and ended his ups and downs; in and out life by being crucified upside down but the Holy Spirit never left him (John 21:18-19).

Thus, it is with us also. We are weak, unworthy; prone to blunder into sin, yet the Lord loves us and forgives us when we go to Him in repentance. The Holy Spirit strives with us, encourages us, and lifts us up when we fall. This is how it will ever be until the Lord calls us home and we see Him face to face. All the time and we waited for the **3 P's** – the **Promise, Power and Pentecost.** If you are not sure about your commitment for waiting for these 3 "P's" the Promise, Power and Pentecost, please come forward today to the altar and someone will pray with you and give you instruction on how to obtain your Promise, Power and Pentecost experience. God Bless!

CHAPTER SIX

CONSECRATION OF MY FIRST BORN TO THE OFFICE OF A BISHOP

In the King James Version of the Bible in Luke 2:23, you will find these words: (*"As it is written in the law of the Lord, Every male that openeth the womb shall be called holy to the Lord."* Our honoree tonight is a firstborn and according to the Holy Scripture was blessed when he was born. The firstborn's birthright blessing is a biblical, historical fact that has been preserved for several thousand years.

According to the Law of Moses, the term "firstborn" was used literally and figuratively, expressing a relationship, an inheritance, preeminence and privileges. The firstborn son's inheritance was a double portion. He had special privileges as the firstborn male of the family (Deut. 21:17).

God gives honor to the first born male of a family. He blesses them with extra money and prosperity so the oldest could provide for their elderly parents, care for the sisters who've never married, and support the family so its bloodline can continue. This blessing was not against the other children. It was meant as an extra portion of blessing as the firstborn often has extra responsibilities and caregiving obligations. Our honoree has experienced this in his life.

According to the Law, not only is the money noticeably different for the firstborn; also the gifts and talents of the male members of the family ancestry are often found present in the personality of the firstborn son. If the ancestors were great managers of time, material, money, or manpower, the firstborn often has the same qualities. I guess that is why our honoree felt compelled, after reaching the office of a Bishop, to drop his given first name of Marcus and begin using his middle name "Ruel", which is his father's first name. He did so in order to continue the legacy of his father, the late Bishop Ruel McCoy.

It is only fitting that tonight we celebrate the consecration of the giving back to the Lord, the first male offspring of my womb. This firstborn who has a relationship with God, an inheritance from God, preeminence in the world, privileges given to him by God, and instruction from God on how to enroll His people in Heaven in order to possess eternal life.

God called Israel His firstborn son. This communicates the relationship He had with Israel, and the preeminence, privileges, and inheritance He granted the nation. God calls David, who was a type of Christ, His firstborn. This communicates the relationship of David with God, looking forward to the relationship Jesus would have with God.

In the Scripture, God uses the term "firstborn" to communicate several things about Jesus and Christians. Jesus is the firstborn of all creation. Jesus is the firstborn from the dead. In other words, He was first to resurrect from the grave; having conquered death. Paul said that Jesus was the firstborn among many brethren. Since Jesus is the firstborn, His Church is called "church of the firstborn." We, as members of the Church triumphant, also have the same blessings from the Lord. Tonight, let us count our blessings, name them one by one, count our many blessings as we see what God has done.

43

BLEST. BROKEN. GIVEN.

CHAPTER SEVEN

THE BOTTOM OF THE BARREL BLESSINGS

RESPONDING TO GOD'S WORD
I Kings 17:8-16, Luke 4:25-26

The widow of Zarephath did, *in faith*, what Elijah asked her to do, and *God met her every need!*

This widow, whose name is never given, lived in Sarepta, which belonged to King Zidon, Jezebel's father. When Israel was unsafe, Elijah found a welcome refuge in this heathen country. Ironically, it was the home of Jezebel, from whom he was fleeing.

Here, Elijah was directed by God, to stay with a widow. Though she lived in a pagan land, it seems she knew something of the faith of the Hebrews before Elijah came to stay. No doubt, she learned even more about God as Elijah sojourned with her in her poor home.

The widow had a child to care for. She was able to work out a frugal living with a few olive trees and a small barley field. When famine struck, she didn't know where the next meal would come from and whether she and her son would live. Little did the distressed widow realize that deliverance was at hand in the form of a rough-looking stranger who appeared at her door.

When Elijah met the widow, she was gathering sticks to make a final scanty meal. Once this meal was eaten, there would be nothing to do but await death by starvation. *But when Elijah told her to go on with the preparation of what she thought would be her last meal,* she obeyed him. She even served him first, as he asked.

Hope must have filled her heart when she saw fresh meal and the empty oil cruse refilled every time she needed something to eat. I don't believe that the barrel and the oil vessel were running over full all the time but whenever she needed meal and oil, she would reach into the barrel and on the bottom of the barrel was the meal. When she poured oil came out of the empty jar.

This widow is an example of one who had *faith to believe that, if she* obeyed *what she was asked to do,* the WORD given would come to pass. She acted before she saw any results. This is the *faith* of Hebrews 11:1, which says, *"Now faith is the substance of things hoped for, the evidence of things not seen."* When the widow heard the word which the Lord spoke through Elijah, she was given *faith* to believe for a miracle.

Romans 10:17 says: *"faith cometh by hearing, and hearing by the word of God."* Hearing the Word is what gives us *faith,* for faith is a gift of God, not something we can muster up ourselves.

The importance of *faith* can't be minimized. Here's why:

- We can't be saved without *faith.* John 3:36; Luke 7:50

- We can't live victoriously over the world without faith. 1 John 5:4

- We can't please God without *faith.* Hebrews 11:6

- We can't pray without *faith.* James 1:6

- We can't have peace with God without *faith.* Romans 5:1

- We're justified by *faith,* not by works. Galatians 2:16

- We're to live by *faith.* Galatians 2:20

- We're made righteous by *faith.* Romans 10:1-4

- Christ dwells in our hearts by *faith.* Ephesians 3:17

- The Holy Spirit is received by *faith.* Galatians 3:2

- Whatever isn't of *faith* is sin! Romans 14:23

Along with *faith,* comes <u>obedience.</u> Obedience is an expression of one's *faith.* The widow of Zarephath could have said, "Yes, I have faith that the oil will increase as I pour it." But her faith would never have become reality until she actually did what she believed. Obedience is the works of James 2:17-26 which makes faith live.

Let's review the widow of Zarephath in light of her *obedience by faith.* When Elijah arrived at her home, he made some unusual requests:

1. He asked for water in a land undergoing a drought

2. He asked for bread when there was only enough oil and meal to make one last meal for the widow and her son.

3. He didn't seem to be suffering from malnutrition; he'd just come from the brook Cherith, where he was fed by ravens.

We each have a choice as to **HOW WE RESPOND TO GOD'S WORD**. If our heart is hard, the Word won't take root and grow. If we're open to God, His Word can accomplish much in us. However, like the widow of Zarephath, we must take the Word by faith and act upon it. This is why we *must* depend upon the Spirit of God to open and unveil the Word of God to us. We must allow Him to give us the *gift of faith,* which is mixed with the Word (logos) and then becomes Rhema to us. As we act upon this word in faith, we have fulfillment. The Word gives us faith, and faith brings the Word to pass! Logos is something said (or thought) - past tense. This is essentially God's written Word, applicable to everyone as His truth. The Rhema Word of God is an utterance - present tense. It's the Word of God (logos) which has been quickening by the Holy Spirit. In the Rhema Word, we find God's personal Word to us for a specific situation. As we received it by faith and act upon it, we are assured it will come to pass.

DO YOU HAVE ENOUGH FAITH TO RECEIVE YOUR <u>BOTTOM OF THE BARREL BLESSINGS?</u>

CHAPTER EIGHT

TRIBUTES TO MY CHILDREN: *LUCAS, DORCAS, AND PRECIOUS*

Proverbs 22:6
"Train up a child in the way he should go; and when he is old, he will not depart from it."

MY SON LUCAS

On November 20, 1963, my second son was born, which was during the time of the assassination of President J. F. Kennedy. The world was in an uproar. When his father told me that he had selected and recorded his name on the birth certificate as Luke Bartholomew McCoy, I said, "Why you didn't write "Lucas" so his name would rhyme with his older brother's name, "Marcus?" Unfortunately, we never changed the name on his birth certificate. We continued to call him Lucas until he entered college; even though that was not the name he was given at birth. During his college freshmen orientation class, he was instructed that he had to use the name "Luke" because that was his legal name and not "Lucas."

His entrance into this world was remarkable. I did not realize that it was time for me to give birth. Before I came home from the hospital, the doctor told his father that Lucas was born with sickle cell anemia and if he lived to be two years old, he would never see his twelfth birthday. He is approaching his fiftieth birthday. He has been married for over 26 years to my wonderful daughter-in-love, Elaine. Together, they have given me

49

two beautiful grandchildren, Luke Jr., and Lukeeshaa. To God, we give the Glory.

His middle name Bartholomew's interpretation is Nathaniel, which means, "no guile found in his mouth." His name truly describes his character and lifestyle. His smile and personality light up any room and situation. He comes to visit me every day and kisses me each time.

He is not Mr. Fix It." He does not even try. His key words to me are: "Mama call the repairman and I'll help you pay for it." I have called on the repairperson "Jesus" many times and Lucas has always been by my side. Once he went on a school trip, he brought me back a statue of two people embracing and on the bottom; the inscription is "Together We Can Solve Anything." That's how I feel about my son" Lucas."

MY DAUGHTER DORCAS
A Women's Day Speech, which describes my
daughter's generosity and tenacity

My husband and I agreed before we had children that he would select the names for our sons, and I would select the names for our daughters. After the birth of my last son, who was born with sickle cell, we were advised to not have any more children because they would have to live in constant pain. When I became pregnant, the doctor therefore advised me to terminate the pregnancy. My husband left the decision up to me. I said, "No, maybe this one will be a girl."

I studied all the female names in the bible and their meanings. The Biblical name *"Dorcas"* and her life's story stuck out. Eventually, I had to change doctors and I selected one in the next town. I stayed prayerful for a healthy daughter and turned my situation over to the Lord. He gave me the desires of my heart. I carried my daughter full term. She only weighed 5 pounds and she came into this world "fighting to live." We came home from the hospital in two days. Dorcas was born with the sickle cell trait and an allergy to dust, but she has never gone through a crisis. It has been an uphill journey, but the Lord has always been present. Her name means gazelle, which is a small, swift antelope with soft, bright eyes, noted for graceful movements. Graceful describes Dorcas perfectly. There are no words in my vocabulary to fully express my love for her and all that she means to me. The following is a Women's Day speech depicting the background and essence of the life of Dorcas in the Bible:

A disciple named Tabitha lived in the city of Joppa. Her Greek name was Dorcas. She always helped people and gave things to the poor. She became sick and died. Her body was prepared for burial and was laid in an upstairs room. Lydda is near the city of Joppa. When the disciples heard that Peter was in Lydda, they sent two men to him. They begged Peter, "Hurry to Joppa! We need your help!" So Peter went with them. When he arrived, he was taken upstairs. All the widows stood around him. They were crying and showing Peter the articles of clothing that Dorcas had made while she was still was alive. Realizing that wasn't not about them, but it was about Jesus; Peter made everyone leave the room. He knelt and prayed. Then he turned toward the body and said, **"Tabitha, get up!"** Tabitha opened her eyes, saw Peter, and sat up. Peter took her hand and helped her stand. After he called the believers; especially the widows, he presented Tabitha to them. She was alive. The news about this spread throughout the city of Joppa, and as a result, many people believed in the Lord.

The fruit of the spirit goodness and love could clearly be seen in Dorcas' life:

- She was a disciple, a faithful follower of Christ who was full of **good works!** She helped the poor, she sewed clothes, and she assisted the widows. She gave of herself **sacrificially; not to be seen by others, but rather to glorify God.**

Galatians 6:10

"As we have therefore opportunity, let us do good unto all [men], especially unto them who are of the household of faith."

- Dorcas' kindness towards others was a testament to her faith. Women of God, we must remember that God will use our good works to benefit others and bring glory to Him.

Mathew 5:16

"Let your light shine before men, that they may see your good deeds and praise your Father which is in heaven."

John 13:35

"For by this shall all men know that you are my disciples, that you have loved one for another?"

- Dorcas **loved** the Lord and she loved all of humanity. Her love was not just spoken, but it was shown.

I John 3:18

"Dear children, let us not love with words or tongue, but with actions and truth."

- God has equipped each of us with gifts we can use to serve Him. Like Dorcas, we must love our neighbors as ourselves. We must keep striving! We must maintain our place on the front line for Jesus. We must never forget that we are soldiers! Faith, prayer and the Word are our weapons of warfare. Challenges and circumstances may come, but this is not the time to die. We must stand firm and allow our love for Jesus to multiply!

Proverbs 31:31

"Give her the fruit of her hands and let her own works praise her in the gates".

- Use your faith, fingers and funds to win the battle in drawing others to Him! You are soldier![1]

---

[1] Excerpts from "I'm A Soldier in the Army of God" poem, author unknown.

I'm not telling you anything new. You know what to do. You've been taught by the Holy Spirit, trained by experience, tried by adversity and tested by fire! Sickness attempted to kill Tabitha's work. But through faith in God, death couldn't keep her in the ground! Women of God, we must have the same determination!

Like Dorcas, you must say to yourself: "I am a volunteer in this army of goodness, kindness and love." I am enlisted for eternity. I will either retire at the rapture or die on the battlefield for my Lord, but I will not get out, sell out, be talked out or pushed out!

Tell the enemy that you refuse to sit on your God given gifts and talents. I don't know about you, but no one has to beg me to work for the Lord. I am not a baby. I don't need to be pampered, petted, primed, pumped, picked up or pepped up! Like Dorcas, I am a soldier.

If the Lord needs me in Sunday school, to teach children, or at the back door to usher, to help the elderly, or just sit, shut my mouth, listen and learn. I am available; He can use me, because like Dorcas, I can say:

"No one has to call me, or cause me to recollect, or inform me, or send me a letter, entice or lure me because I am a soldier. I know who holds my destiny and is the captain of my soul. I've completed Basic Training. I know my rank and what is required of me: to do justly, to love mercy, and to walk humbly with my God, praising His name and obeying His orders."

Like Dorcas, I have been chosen and I am committed. My feelings cannot be hurt enough to stop me from serving my Master. Discouragement cannot turn me aside. Nothing can cause me to give up and quit. When Jesus called my number for enlisting in His Army, I was a nobody; now I'm a child of the King with an inheritance. God has not given me the spirit of fear but of power, love and a sound mind!

Like Dorcas, I will win in the end. I will continue to serve others by denying myself. I know my God is a promise keeper and He promised He would supply all of my needs. I am victorious and can do all things through Christ who gives me strength.

Satan cannot defeat me, the world cannot disillusion me, the storms of life cannot weary me, wars cannot beat me, no amount of money can buy me, governments can't shut me up, illness can't stop me, and no grave can hold my body down. As you learned from my story, in the book of Acts, even death couldn't destroy me.

When the King of Kings calls me from this battlefield, He will reward me, promote me and then bring me back to rule this world with Him, because I am a soldier in His army. I am a witness for Him as I march on, claiming victory, and telling the good news of His death, burial and resurrection.

Like Dorcas, you can also be presented alive. Stand up if you want to be a soldier! Heels together, stomach in, chest out, chin up and eyes opened wide with pride! You will march forward and never backwards! Like Dorcas, are you on Active Duty; do you serve the Lord faithfully each day, without murmuring and disputing? Or, are you on Reserved Status: Waiting to return because you allowed someone to kill your joy? Perhaps you have been so hurt that you missed it when Peter through the word of God came by to speak life into your soul. I say to you **DORCAS ARISE!**

You cannot afford to be AWOL: Absent without the Lord! Today is your day to recommit to the service of the Lord. **Dorcas Arise!!!** You are a soldier! He gave you blessed hands to reach out to man; to show him God's love and His perfect plan. Like Dorcas, let a revival begin with you! Help somebody along the way so your living won't be in vain. Your talent doesn't have to put you on the front row. Whatever it is that God has given you, serve with all your mind, body and soul. Even if they never call your name; remember: it's not about us, it's about Jesus! **Arise Dorcas!**

He was wounded for our transgression; He was bruised for our iniquity. The chastisement of our peace was upon Him and by His stripes we are healed! Your depression is healed. Your low self-esteem is healed. Your shyness is healed. Your finances are healed. **Arise Dorcas!** Death can't keep you in the ground. What can separate us from the love of God which is in

Christ Jesus? **Arise Dorcas!** You are a soldier and you have been **called** to serve for such a time as this!

MY DAUGHTER
PRECIOUS

In 1981 while attending a meeting in Lakeland, Florida, a sister in Christ approach me and said, "Mother McCoy, I have a granddaughter that I can't really see about. My daughter brought her home to me and I am already taking care of her two boys. She is such a pretty baby. Do you want her? I replied, "Yes, but let me check with my husband and family and I'll get back with you."

I could not wait to discuss it with my family. I was so happy. I was forty-three years old, my oldest son was in college, my second son was a senior in high school, and my daughter was in the 9th grade. We agreed that to have a baby in the house would be enjoyable for all of us. My husband and I returned to Lakeland the following weekend to pick her up. Her name was Aprielle Sophia Williams. She was five months old, chubby, beautiful, with dark velvety skin and a mole on her nose. She also had a head full of curly hair. She immediately became the love of our lives. I made her a birth certificate and changed her name to Precious in order to have the "us" and "as" sound to rhyme with the other children's names. I was able to enroll her in school, get insurance and receive all the benefits just as if I had given birth to her. She was a happy child and brought joy into our home.

In 1985, my husband became ill; he died in 1993. The financial aspect of our home changed greatly. All of my birth children were too old for state assistance, but because of Precious, we qualified for the help that we so much needed. At my husband's demise, I was fifty- five and Precious was twelve. I legally adopted her and her legal name became Precious Aprielle McCoy. She was able to receive to my husband's social security benefits, just as if he was her biological father. She and I received a check

59

until she became eighteen years old and I was sixty-two. This is how we were able to survive until I was old enough to draw social security from my husband's work record. If it were not for Precious, I do not know how we would have survived after the death of my husband. To God be the Glory. Thank God for putting Precious in our lives when He did. When I said "Yes I want a baby; someone that I can care for, protect and love," I did not know that that one day our roles would be reversed.

Precious lives in our first family home. The children did not want to sell it because of the memories we shared with their father growing up there. Precious loves to shop and always remembers me. She does not wait for special occasions. On any average day, Precious will drive up with a new item she has purchased for her Mother. I am grateful for my God-given daughter, who is the essence of her name, Precious.

BLEST. BROKEN. GIVEN.

CHAPTER NINE

WE NEED EACH OTHER TO SURVIVE
"...Am I my brother's keeper?" Psalm 4:9

The fourth chapter of Ephesians tells us about the unity of the Spirit. In that believers are one in the Spirit, it is our duty to keep the unity, recognize it, and act upon it without demonstrating a denominational spirit.

"I need you, you need me, we're all a part of God's body, stand with me, agree with me, we're all a part of God's body. It is His will that our needs be supplied. You're important to me, I need you to survive. I pray for you, you pray for me, I love you, I need you to survive. I won't harm you with words from my mouth, I love you! I need you to survive."

Survive means to remain alive; to live on, to continue to exist; to live longer than; to outlast. A survivor is something that lives on or lasts after others like it have gone. You have to go through something to be called a survivor. In order to survive, we must do all we can to keep harmony and oneness of the Spirit in the binding power of peace. We may be many members, but we are still just one body and that one body has only one spirit. He that hath not the Spirit of God, does not belong to Him.

Sisters, we must walk in love just as Christ also loved us. He gave Himself for us, an offering and a sacrifice to God as a fragrant aroma. For we walk by faith, not by sight. Therefore, be careful how you walk; not as unwise women, but as wise women of God. But if we walk in the light as He Himself is in the light, we have fellowship with one another, and the Blood of Jesus cleanses us from all sin. I, therefore, entreat you to walk in a manner worthy of the calling with which you have been called.

We are living in the Laodicea Church Age, where the worldly influences have crept into the church, and produced a lukewarm spirit within. People want to do anything, wear anything and still confess to be a child of the King. Sisters, in order to survive and see that the next generation also survives; we must unify ourselves in our teaching and living.

We need unity. We must teach the unadulterated Truth, the divine Word of God according to the Bible, rather than our personal opinions. God is calling for pure holiness and nothing less. We can hear people saying, "Times have changed and you have to change with the times." Yes, I agree that times have changed, but God has not changed. He said in His Word that He changes not (Mal. 3:6). He's the same yesterday, today and forever (Heb. 13:8).

We are approaching the coming of the Lord, and in order to make the rapture, we must survive. It's so much easier when we work together. Encourage you sister, lift her up in prayer. Show her love, be patient and kind, be forgiving, and if she should just happen to fall, extend your hand out to her and lift her up. Always remember that we are women of the light and stand united. Together we stand and divided we will fall. We must work together for the perfecting of the Body of Christ.

Matthew 23:37-40 Jesus said, *"Thou shalt love the Lord, they God with all thy heart, and with all thy soul, and with all thy mind. This is the first and great commandment. And the second is like unto it, Thou shalt love thy neighbor as thyself. On these two commandments hang all the law and the prophets."* The question Cain asked long ago, *"Am I my brother's keeper?"* Jesus answered, "Yes"! We are to be one, just like Him and His Father.

It is recorded in St. John 17:20-23, *"Neither pray I for these alone, but for them also which shall believe on me*

through their word; That they all may be one; as thou,
Father, art in me, and I in thee, that they also may be one in
us: that the world may believe that thou hast sent me. And
the glory which thou gavest me I have given them; that they
may be one, even as we are one: I in them, and thou in me,
that they may be made perfect in one; and that the world
may know that thou hast sent me, and hast loved them, as
thou hast loved me."

Jesus, not only prayed for the unity and the future glory of those whom the Father had given Him, but for all future believers, as well. In order for us to be victorious, to unite, teaching the Word of God and reaching the world for Christ, we must work together and strengthen our sisters on this journey.   We must be mindful of all things, elevate our minds, and encourage ourselves as we encourage others. Therefore, my beloved sisters, let us be steadfast unmovable always abounding in the work of the Lord, knowing that our toiling is not in vain.

The Apostolic Woman who lives by the Word, shows compassion towards her sister. Ephesians 4:1-3 tells us that Jesus has called us to walk worthy of the vocation wherewith we are called. With all lowliness and meekness, with longsuffering, forbearing one another in love, we are to endeavor to keep the unity of the spirit in the bonds of peace. I believe that the Lord wants us to obey and follow leadership that will take us where He wants us to be. There is only one vision. It is a vision that blesses people. Believe in the words of the prophets and thou shall live and prosper (II Chronicles 20:20). *"For without a vision the people will perish" (Proverbs 29:18).*

II Chronicles 7:14 states *"If my people, which are called by my name, shall humble Themselves, and pray, and seek my face, and turn from their wicked ways; then will I hear from heaven, and will forgive their sin, and will heal their land."*

God knows His plan and He is working all things out in accordance to His purpose. The Godly women are responsible to study and proclaim His revelation while awaiting its fulfillment. As daughters of the Most High, we must be attentive to the Word of God. The Word is our ultimate judge. In Colossians 2:2, Paul encourages us to have true intimacy with the Lord as well as with each other. We must see ourselves, not as solitary individuals, but as important and cherished member of Christ's body. We are daughters of Sarah—children of the King. When we identify ourselves as God's, then we can work together without the interference of pride, greed, envy or any such thing. Obedience is necessary for survival.

We all need a companion in our "desert," but more than that, we need a Shepherd. *I need you and you need me, we're all a part of God's Body. It is God's will that our needs be supplied. You're important to me. I pray for you and you pray for me. I love you. I won't harm you with words from my mouth.* We need each other to survive. Hallelujah! Praise the Lord for your sister in Christ. As sisters, we should love one another into the Kingdom of God. A sister is a girl or woman related to a person by having the same parents. A sister may also be defined as members of a religious society of women.

Look at the word **UNITY**. It is **U, N, I,** knowing **Y** *(You and I knowing why)*. Unity is based on the word unit that means entity. Think about that, you could say that unity is a unit with the "y". United means (you and I tied together). The word unity is only mentioned in the Bible three times. I believe that unity is you and your sister knowing why you do things. Knowing why enables you to be a unit for God's use. Isn't it easier for us to use one object at a time? Therefore, it is important for us to strive for UNITY in the church, so that God can use us more effectively.

It is recorded in Psalms 133:1 (A song degree of David), "*Behold, how good and how pleasant it is for brethren to dwell together in unity.*" The UNITY mentioned here means fellowship, people, or altogether.

Ephesians 4:3 states "*Endeavor to keep the Unity of the Spirit in the bonds of peace.*" Here UNITY means agreement, spirit, or communion.

Ephesians 4:13 tell us, "*Till we all come in the Unity of the faith, and of the knowledge of the Son of God, unto a perfect man, unto the measure of the stature of the fullness of Christ.*" Here UNITY means divinity, or faith.

Sisters, we need each other to survive. Unity comes from our walk; therefore we are to walk with humility, with all gentleness, patience and love. We are to work hard at maintaining unity in the bond of peace. Unity comes from holding things in common. We must be on the same page with the same goals. The Disciples' only goal was spreading the Gospel. We may have different opinions, but we must come together on certain things. We are one Body, Spirit, Lord, Faith, Baptism and One God.

Beloved, unity comes from our functioning in the body, according to our giftedness. Each of us has been given at least one spiritual gift because we have to be equipped for the work of service. Only three things can happen in a church: (1) the believers are not equipped so they cannot serve properly; (2) they are equipped, but never serve; or (3) they are equipped and they build up the body of Christ. We are to use our gifts to build up the body and not tear it down. As we build up the body, we build ourselves into mature believers. Unity comes when we decide to no longer be children. We have a unity of beliefs that gives us a mature knowledge of Christ. Paul says that we should grow up in all aspects to Christ. We should be like Him—the expressed image of Him. Christ is working in us, causing growth, so that we are building up the Church in love.

The Lord hath in Himself: All power to defend us All wisdom to direct us All mercy to pardon us All grace to enrich us, All righteousness to clothe us All goodness to supply us, and All happiness to crown us.

Run my sister for your reward is ahead of you. **Sing** my daughters of Zion, for your joy is hidden in your song. **Weep** my wailing women for God will wipe away all tears. **Love** my sisters, for love is the power of our strength. **Pray** my sisters, for prayer will prepare the way of the journey and corresponding victory that is ahead of us. Remember we need each other to survive. Unity is our theme and Glory in our unified goal.

SURVIVAL KIT

A RUBBER BAND is to remind us that God has promised to enlarge our coast. (1 Chronicles 4:10)

A piece of TISSUE is to remind us that God called for the wailing women. (Jeremiah 9:20)

A BAND AID is to remind us that "By His Stripes We Are Healed." (Isaiah 53:6; 61:12)

A TOOTH PICK is to remind us to pick out good qualities in everyone. (Philippians 2:2-4)

A BUTTONS is to remind us to button our lips. (Psalms 5:3; Colossians 3:9; Joshua 3:5, 6)

A MINT is to remind us that a soul is worth a mint to us. (Matthew 5:14)

A LIFE SAVER is to remind us that Jesus is still in the soul-saving business. (Acts 2:38)

An ERASER is to remind us that God erases our slate and gives us a new slate. (I John 21:1-2)

A TEA BAG is to remind us to relax daily and go over our list of blessings. (Psalms 103:1)

A stick of CHEWING GUM is to remind us to stick with it. (Philippians 1:6)

A PENCIL is to remind us to write the vision and make it plain. (Habakkuk 2:2)

A SAFETY PIN – To remind us that we must go through to come out. (I Peter 5:10.)

As President of the IWC, I passed out safety pins to remind the Women of God that in order for that pin to be useful, it must go through something and come out, and then be closed for protection. We must go through and come out, believing that we are going to hold fast in afflictions, in temptations, and in the midst of storms.

CHAPTER TEN

MY "RECOVERY" TESTIMONY

"But he was wounded for our transgressions, he was bruised for our iniquities; the chastisement of our peace was upon him; and with his stripes we are healed." Isaiah 53:5

I am glad I had a personal relationship with the Lord when (Isaiah 53:5) became a reality in my life. *"...and with His stripes we are healed."* After walking with Him for over fifty years, in April of 2005, at the age of 67, I was diagnosed with an inoperable brain tumor about the size of the point of a pencil. I was told that it would take away my memory and the ability to create. I was told many people suffer with this condition and adjust. I was told to daily do exercises to stimulate my brain cells. The main recommended activity was to count backward from one hundred by sevens.

The neurologists gave me a prescription that was supposed to control the seizures. I threw the medicine out of the car window on my way home. I felt that the Lord had slowed me down and He truly got my attention. However, I was devastated! I didn't want to live without my memory. So, I did all that I could possibly do to hold on to it. After a period of time, doing puzzles did not satisfy that inward desire to conquer the battle to preserve my mind.

One day in prayer and meditation, the Lord dropped in my soul the desire to spend more time studying His Word. I memorized many Scriptures, including whole chapters. I recited the Word daily, but I still wasn't satisfied. I had such a thirst to learn more about Jesus that I decided to enroll in the W. L. Bonner Bible College in Columbia, South Carolina. It is an accredited college which offers an on-site Institute Program on its campus one week out of the month. Each month, for three and one half years, I rode the train from Florida to South Carolina in pursuit of my degree. Finally, in June of 2008, at the age of 70, I graduated as salutatorian of my graduating class from the W. L. Bonner Bible College. I earned the Bachelor of Studies in Women Ministries. In 2011 at the age of 73, I earned a Masters of Theological Studies from Liberty University. At age 75, I will graduate with an EdS, educational specialist, and plan to continue for the EdD, doctorate of education.

Of course, I am claiming my healing, but the devil is busy and very good at his job by bringing doubt to my mind. I must remember that in the aging process, one's memory is sometimes the first to go. So, when I can't remember things, I remind myself that it's not the tumor; but old age. I still would like to grow old gracefully. I am committed to doing what the Lord requires of me "… to do justly, and to love mercifully, and to walk humbly with thy God" (Micah 6:8). I'm holding Him to His promises. Lord, you promised that if I walk upright before you, that there is nothing you would withhold from me.

By putting my thoughts in this writing, I can see how much I used the word "I". Now, I must fully turn this situation over to the Lord and allow Him to deliver me through the many challenging issues of life. Yes, it is good to reach the lost in sharing our testimonies, but sometimes it is necessary to "revive" one's self in order to become an effective witness. To me, recovery means to get something back in return so I do feel that this is a "recovery" testimony in that I have rediscovered God's plan for my life.

I can truly say that I know the Lord as a healer because He has manifested Himself so many times in my life and even through my family. If He doesn't deliver me from this affliction, I still know that He is able. All sickness is not until death; but for His glorification.

BLEST. BROKEN. GIVEN.

CHAPTER ELEVEN

THE JOY OF THE LORD COMES IN "CANS"

"I Can Do All Things through Christ that Strengthens Me" – Phil. 4:13

The first International Women's Council of the Church of Our Lord Jesus Christ of the Apostolic Faith, Inc., convened in October of 1952 in Petersburg, Virginia. The Council has met every October since 1952. The Theme for the 1952 meeting was *"Let Us Arise and Build a House."* The Motto was Philippians 4:13, "I **can** do all things through Christ which strengtheneth me." The slogan was: *"Workers for Christ."* The Late Mother Perry stated that her theme was "UNITY" and her goal was "GLORY" and with God's help, she would realize her desire.

When I became the ninth president of this great Women's Auxiliary, I adopted Mother Perry's Theme for my administration. Over 60 years later, the women of God of the Church of Our Lord are still working for Christ building His house and still voicing the same sentiments as our ancestors. We believe as a Paul did, "We **can** still do all things through Christ which gives us strength." Say within you, "I **can** do all things through Christ who gives me strength. I am connected to Christ, and because I am connected to Christ, He lives in me, and the life which I live, is His life, living through me."

Paul was a prisoner in Rome when he wrote Philippians 4:13. He had lost his freedom and all of the comforts that it affords. In order to help him with his life in prison, the Philippians had sent him a gift. He thanked them, said he had learned to be content and find joy in whatever his circumstances were. After all that he had been through, he still counted it all joy.

"I can do all things." Paul uses a Greek verb, *ischuros* that means to be strong or to have strength. He is saying, "I am strong enough to go through anything because of He, Who infuses His strength into me. In the latter clause…**"through Christ who strengtheneth me,"** the word "strengthened" *endunamoo,* means put power in or to infuse with power. The Lord infuses us with strength and power. He puts it in us, when we are at our extremities. Paul is saying, "I have the power, authority and strength to go through all things." He has the ability to deal with all kinds of material circumstances because of his spiritual strength. He knew that the Lord was able to remove him from any situation or prepare him to be steadfast in any situation.

Beloved, what brings real joy and contentment is when we have learned not to depend upon our resources. When we have been to the desert or in the valley; when we have been to our extremity; when we have walked in the valley and the shadow of death; when we have been on the brink of no return or we have come to the point where we are out of resources, we **CAN** turn to the Lord, and find the strength that we need to go through any difficulty. I can say with blessed assurance, that this is the true secret of joy and contentment.

We can say like Paul because I have strength and power on the inside. I **can** go without food, for a while; I **can** go with clothes; I **can** go without comfort; I **can** go without warmth; I **can** go without freedom; I **can** go without care; I **can** endure suffering; I **can** endure pain; I **can** endure threats; I **can** endure all of that on the outside because I am strengthened with power on the inside. I serve the Lord, from the inside to the outside. I have been brought with a price; I am no longer my own. I **can** be led, not driven. I will take His yoke upon me and learn of Him because His yoke is easy and His burdens are light.

A yoke is a bar or frame of wood which fits over the necks of two animals, such as oxen, and holds them together, for pulling a load. It is two who are joined at the neck. Jesus, is saying, Come unto me, attach yourself with me in this yoke and let's plow together and break-up whatever is put before us as we rejoice, with joy and contentment, in the God of our salvation.

In Philippians 4:13, Paul writes, "I am praying that you will be strengthened with power through His spirit in the inner man, and when we are strengthened with power through His spirit, in the inner man we are able to do exceeding, abundantly beyond all we ask or think according to that power." In other words, we, as believers, have a resource within us, which is the life of God. It is a power source that **can** sustain us when we don't imagine it will.

The Lord has told every one of His children that, "Nothing is impossible or too hard for Him." Let us take the limits off of the Lord. He also said, "I've come that you might have life and have it more abundantly.**"** Why not get a life? The Lord hath in Himself all *power* to defend us, all *wisdom* to direct us, all *mercy* to pardon us; all *grace* to enrich us, all *righteousness* to clothes us, all *goodness* to supply us, and all *happiness/joy* to crown us.

You see, when we get to the point where we are at the end of our resources and we are wholly dependent on the Lord so that we **can** see the movement of His power, we will find joy in **"I can."** I **can** do something. We must use this power, dynamite and strength that are within us so we can magnify and glorify our Maker.

The joy of the Lord comes in **"CANS."** We cannot go to the supermarket to buy this **can**. We need to develop the **"I can" mentality.** I **can** do all things because the Lord Almighty is with me and He is in me—and greater is He that is in me than he that is in the world. I **can** climb this impossible mountain. I **can** walk thru this agonizing moment that I am experiencing because of God's grace: His unmerited favor toward undeserving men. We must believe true contentment is being able to be satisfied and content in the midst of any problem. That's the kind of joy we must have through Jesus Christ our Lord.

When our trials and temptations come, those of us, who rely on Christ, may be shaken, (perhaps?) but never completely undone. Deep down, even if all we have is a mustard seed of faith, that seed is connected to the ROCK. That ROCK is steadfast, and unmovable; so those who trust in Him will be steadfast, secured, rooted and protected.

It's recorded in John 10:27-29, *"My Sheep hear my voice, and I know them, and they follow me, and I give eternal life to them, and they will never perish, and no one will snatch hem out of my hand. My father, who has given them to me, is greater than all, and no one is able to snatch them out of the Father's hand."*

In order for Satan to get to the believers, we would have to be pried out of the Lord's own hand; which will never happen. We are safe; therefore, why not be content with a joyful heart?

We are in a spiritual warfare and may come out bloody and with scars. However, we must put on the whole armor of God so that we'll be able to *"withstand"* the fiery darts of the Devil. We, therefore, through Christ, must cast evil out of our lives and cast all of our cares upon Him.

Remember we can't pray for strength to do anything—the joy of the Lord is our strength and joy comes in **"CANS."**

Jesus was wounded, bruised, beaten and scourged as an example of suffering and brokenness, for the salvation or wholeness of the world. He endured a Crown of Thorns while it was painfully thrust into His head. Huge spikes were driven through His hands and feet, He suffered severe beatings, stripes on His back, and a sword pierced through His side, through which His Blood was shed for the cleansing of our sins. Like Jesus, we have to take up our cross—His Yoke—bear it and follow His directions. One of our greatest endeavors should be to know the Lord.

Jeremiah 9:23 states, *"Thus saith the Lord, Let not the wise man glory in his wisdom, neither let the might man glory in his might, let not the rich man glory in his riches: But let him that glorieth, glory in this, that he understandth and knoweth me, that I'm the Lord which exercise loving kindness, judgment, and righteousness, in the earth: For in these things I delight, saith the Lord."*

Recorded in Hosea 6:3 are these words, *"Then shall we know, if we follow on to know the LORD; His going forth is prepared as the morning: and He shall come unto us as the rain, as the latter and former rain unto the earth."*

To know the Lord, is to know victory, joy, peace and love. Joy comes from the Lord. To know means to communicate with Him or to talk with Him in the Spirit, in your secret closet. When we come to know the Lord, no mountain is too high or no weapon formed against us will prosper. When we are blessed, no one can curse us. All we need is to know the Lord and we **can** do all things thru Him that gives us strength. When we really know the Lord, the Devil will not be able to confuse us. We **can** come to know the Lord in the power of His suffering.

It is recorded in Romans 5:3: *"Because we should glory in tribulation knowing that tribulations worketh patience and patience, experience and experience hope; and hope maketh is not ashamed because the love of God is shed aboard in our heart by the Holy Ghost which is given unto us."*

The Holy Spirit searches the deep things about God. We must learn to pray in the Spirit. The Holy Spirit visits us through our mind; our strength is our thought. Don't limit the Holy Spirit because it **can** take us into a world of mysteries and put us in contact with the Lord. The Holy Spirit will never leave us nor forsake us. Beloved, He will always be with us until the end of the world. So count it all joy when you fall into divers (various, different) temptations, knowing that the trying of your faith works patience. Our brokenness is neither designed to maim nor damage us, but to build character, integrity, honesty, dignity, and sensitivity. Without the spirit of brokenness, we will never be humble enough to yield ourselves as effective servants for the Lord; because the Lord gives His grace to the humble. Remember, the Lord we serve is able to bear us up when we stumble. We have someone to lean on when we feel weak. Say within yourself; "Come now Lord. Reveal yourself to me". I have to get to know you, understand you and glorify you. If you want to be fruitful, try spending more time in the valley and thank God for Jesus Christ, knowing you **can** conquer all things because it takes valleys to make mountains. Know that you are more than a conqueror.

Regardless of our tests, trials, rejections and tribulations, God expects us to live Holy. He left us the Holy Ghost which supplies everything we need to lead and guide us in the path of righteousness. We have the Grace of God and His favor, to overcome whatever is before us. Yes, we are on a mission; this world is not our home, but it's a fixed fight. It is not necessary to run on to see what the end will be, because we **can** hold the Lord to His promise that He that endures to the end, shall receive eternal life. Let us expect great things from the Lord and seek do great things in Him. Let us live a victorious life, remembering that we *cannot* be defeated because we **can** do all things through Christ which gives us strength. The joy of the Lord is our strength and His joy comes in **"CANS."** If we **can** believe it then we **can** receive it because we are a new creation in Christ Jesus and His anointing is our identification.

BLEST. BROKEN. GIVEN.

CHAPTER TWELVE

LADIES INVOLVED FOR EDUCATION (L-I-F-E)

I CAME THAT THEY MIGHT HAVE *"LIFE"*, AND MIGHT HAVE IT ABUNDANTLY (John 10:10).

Get a life! **L**adies **I**nvolved **for** **E**ducation. I would like to challenge the Apostolic women to continue their process of spiritual discernment by deepening their understanding of their faith and doctrine. It is recorded in the Scripture, (I Peter 3:15): *"But sanctify the Lord God in your hearts: and be ready always to give an answer to every man that asketh you a reason of the hope that is in you with meekness and fear."*

The Lord has blessed the Church of Our Lord Jesus Christ Organization with an accredited Institution of higher learning, to prepare and provide the women of God in this organization with a thorough, critical knowledge of the Bible, its environment and the history of its interpretation.

I wish to express my heartfelt appreciation to the Lord's servant, Bishop William L. Bonner, the founder and President of this institution because of his passion for education and his love of the Lord Jesus Christ. Bishop Bonner has made many, consecrated contributions which have made this work possible.

In 2008, at the age of 70, I graduated after 3 ½ years from this institution. Therefore, I consider myself the voice of experience. I also thought I was a studious Bible scholar because of the length of time I had sat under many who delivered the Gospel. However, while attending this institution I studied the Bible and not Doctrine. Everything wasn't just "black" or "white" but I had to learn about the "gray" areas. The first question that was asked of the students that struck a deep cord was "Is the Holy Spirit a person?" Next, "Does the Holy Spirit have a personality?" Then came the statement: "God was made out of a Thought." My experience at WLBC was very rewarding. I will be eternally grateful that I was allowed to experience such.

When I was the IWC president, I took a busload of twenty-six people to Columbia, South Carolina, every third Saturday, to study at this great institution. The fellowship on the bus was spiritually uplifting.

During this period of time, the death angel took my oldest sister (Mary) and my brother (Yookie). The call about Mary's demise came while I was in class, but my family and friends thought it best to wait to tell me when I was heading back home on the bus. I was surrounded with sincere prayers and love which helped to shield the initial blow.

On that Saturday, my college instructor asked me offer up a "prayer of thanksgiving." I knew my sister was gravely ill. I said within myself, "How can I thank the Lord, when my heart was so heavy?" The more I talked out loudly to the Lord and the more I searched my soul, the lighter my load seemed. Different students in the class took over and also began to cry unto the Lord in prayers of thanksgiving.

Then a Bishop came into the classroom to make an announcement. He heard the wailing for my sister and joined us. He was from New Jersey which was where my sister was hospitalized. He got information on her and said that he would visit her when he returned home. Sadly, she died before he left Columbia. The same time that the prayers were being offered up in Columbia, South

Carolina, was around the time that sister passed in New Jersey. I was told that a "Code Blue" summons went out over the intercom and that the hospital staffed worked on my sister for over 45 minutes. The last time I saw my sister, a nurse said to me, "You've gone as far as you can with sister."

Of course, she was wrong. I still have my sister in my heart to the end of eternity. I'm living with that blessed hope that bye and bye, soon and very soon, we'll be caught up together to meet our Maker in the air because we have **LIFE's** promises and were ladies involved in education.

My late husband used to say, "If you can't go, then send go." Maybe you're not physically or mentally able to accept the challenge to seek a higher education at this time. Then, why not sponsor someone who desires to attend the W. L. Bonner College but is financially unable?

My vision of **LIFE (**L**adies** I**nvolved** F**or** E**ducation)** is that it would be mandated that all Missionaries of the Church of Our Lord Jesus Christ attend the W. L. Bonner College in Columbia, South Carolina before they can receive credentials. The requirements of the missionaries should be the same as the ministers: you must attend the W. L. Bonner College before one receives license in this organization.

The vision also includes the establishment an endowment for the college. This can be done having a fundraiser of a Women's Conference Cruise. We can also sponsor a golf tournament preceding the International Women's Council. The IWC could seek endowments through grants, government, businesses and other fundraising avenues. In the financial obligations of COOLJC, education should be given the same attention (or more) as Evangelism, Foreign Missions, and Home

Missions.

It is my prayer as I commit **(LIFE)** into the hands of our Lord and Savior, Jesus Christ, that the Holy Spirit may use this vision through dedicated Women of God to motivate them to want to study His Word and to glorify the Name that is above every name. I pray that they will lead those who are now in darkness into the Kingdom of God's Dear Son, and bring those who are now carnal minded to a place where they will render a consecrated service to our Matchless Redeemer. Give them the zeal to want the study at WLBC and a sacrificial desire to financially support this effort.

The Bible states in II Timothy 2:15, which we should *"Study to shew thyself approved unto God, a workman that needeth not to be ashamed, rightly dividing the word of Truth."* We must have the ability to provide counsel with attention to the spiritual dimensions, faith issues, and social context of the lives of other women by knowing how to rightly divide the Word of God.

The Bible was written to the Jews, Gentiles and the Church of God. We must be equipped to appropriately interpret the Scripture and recognize the importance of nurturing religious faith and knowledge in all aspects of Ministry. The Holy Scripture states that the Apostolic Women are to teach and take responsibility in directing a variety of aspects to develop and implement the goals that their daughters should strive to attain. The old adage "Give a man a fish and he will eat for a day, teach a man to fish and he'll be able to always eat fish," reminds me of what is recorded in Matthew 13:12: *"Give instruction to a wise man, and he will be get wiser, teach a just man, and he will increase in learning."*

As Ladies Involved for Education **(LIFE),** we must allow our thoughts to open all mysteries for us as we come together, to bind our thoughts, to spread and teach the doctrine and beliefs of COOLJC faith to the up and coming generation. We desire to establish and maintain our own schools, clinics and churches throughout the world. We must hold to our beliefs, teaching and practicing it. We must be alert to the Lord's warning against pride and self-seeking attitudes that can lead to harmful division.

Get a **life!** What really constitutes **life? Life** is a direction or way in which one lives. The majority of us desire to live a good life, so we try treating everyone equally and staying out of harm's way. The truth is, we were born unclean and the way we truly clean ourselves as far as living goes – is simply by carefully reading and studying the map of God's Word and applying it daily to our **life.** It has proven itself from generation to generation. Try it for yourself!

Ladies, we must get involved in educating ourselves and others. We must put feet on our prayers and do something by learning how to release what the Lord has given us to do. Freedom of expression must not bias our understanding. Yes, the principles are the same but the methods we are accustomed to must change.

Many have their own personal meaning of the word "ladies." I have found that if you are a female who has nurtured, shared the Word of God, offered guidance and advice without judging, shown unconditional love, shared wisdom, words of encouragement, simply smiled when someone else did all of the talking, sown love when it was warranted, mentored, corrected a wrong; you are a lady. Maybe you have steered someone over the pitfall, hugged, laughed and cried with someone in good times and bad. Maybe you can admit when you are wrong or simply apologize to teach another that they don't always have to be right. Perhaps, you are fair and consistent. These wonderful traits are, to me, what being a lady is all about.

Ladies (Apostolic women) are responsible to study and proclaim God's revelation while awaiting its fulfillment. Our prayer should be, *"Lord, bless me that I will be able to speak your Word. Anoint the hearers that they will be able to receive the message. Stir up our gifts within that we'll be mindful to lift you up and praise and glorify your Precious Name, as we press toward the mark for the prize of the high calling in Christ Jesus."*

Apostolic women are required to prepare and deliver effective topics, workshops, seminars and to plan and lead various forms of worship. We must have the ability to design and lead learning programs for the development of personal and community faith and **life.** Therefore, we must make an effort to prepare ourselves to do what thus saith the Lord. We must be about our Father's business. We were bought with a price to serve the Lord with gladness of heart. Yes, much study is causes weariness of the flesh, but let us not become weary in doing what is required of us.

Beloved, faith and promises work together to bring about the Will of God. As believers, we are to study the Scriptures as God's Word and by faith we are to accept and believe God's promises to guide and sustain our lives.

Over the entrance of the Bethune-Cookman University which is in my hometown are three words: "Enter to Learn and over the exit is "Depart to Serve." My vision for **LIFE** slogan would read over the entrance "Making Disciples" and over the exit door "Teaching Disciples" (Matthew 28:20). The Theme would be "Work and Wait, Work and Watch, Work and Weigh, Work and Walk."

Think of these things:

- Apostolic women have a duty as Christ's disciples to *"walk worthy of the vocation wherewith ye are called"* (Ephesians 4:14), by denying self and bearing their crosses daily.

- There must be a willingness to study His Word, conform to His Examples and continue in well doing, no matter what obstacles may lie in wait.

- Sacrifice denotes self-denial. Women, in the past as well as today, have practiced and are still practicing the selfless act of sacrificing themselves in a multiplicity of ways, for the sake of others.

- Most of us live and die and never receive God's best things in our lives only because we never gave the Lord our best.

Somehow the world has failed to see the real meaning of salvation. Salvation is an outstanding Bible doctrine and also the initial believer's experience. The Saints of God need to clearly see what the Lord did for the when He died on the cross. Unless we as believer have a clear knowledge of salvation, we cannot receive the adequate benefits that it provides.

Faith is an important and necessary part of every believer's **life.** The Bible says that without faith, it is impossible to please God. Through faith, the Biblical heroes of faith conquered kingdoms, wrought might deeds on behalf of God's people, and were victorious in battle. If we are to reign victoriously over the power of evil, we too must trust, and unconditionally study God's Word.

Please accept this challenge to help the initiation of Ladies Involved For Education (**L.I.F.E**). As they seek a higher education in Biblical Studies, these ladies will commit to raising funds for the W. L. Bonner College in

Columbia, South Carolina. They will also share and dedicate their talents, as well as, give of their time, influence, and means, to study, teach and spread the Gospel at home and abroad.

BLEST. BROKEN. GIVEN.

CHAPTER THIRTEEN

FOLLOWING THE GARBAGE TRUCK

"If we suffer, we shall also reign with him: if we deny him, he also will deny us." **II Timothy 2:12**

My earliest recollection of life is living on Plainfield Avenue in Scotch Plains, New Jersey. I don't know how old I was when our family moved to Westfield, New Jersey to a place that was called "the woods." We rented a small three room house from Mrs. Burton. When we moved my mother only had three children but after a while there were seven children plus my parents in this small house. It's like my mother had two sets of children. After having had three children, she went ten years without having a child; then she had four more.

My sister and I slept in the same bedroom in a double bed. When a new baby arrived, it slept with our parents for a while. Then when the baby was weaned, it was put in a crib in my parent's room. When the baby was older, it went to sleep with the girls (down to the bottom) or into the makeshift bed that our father had attached to the walls for the boys, according to the sex of the baby. Our clothes were on hangers that were placed on nails that were on the walls. We each had a drawer in a big dresser for our underwear.

My father drove us to church; but sometime the pastor or others had to give us a ride home. I was ashamed of where my family lived. Our house was located on a dead end road that led to the "dump". No paved road, no inside plumbing, no mailman or any other delivery truck, but the garbage truck. On Saturday, the iceman would bring a huge chuck of ice and put in the icebox on the porch.

The garbage truck came daily and would dump garbage and rubbish that was collected from stores in the city. I knew the arrival time of the truck and I knew the sound of its motor. Every day when the truck passed my house, I would run behind it as fast as I could so I would be the first kid to look through the stuff. Anything that I thought our family could use I brought home and proudly say, "Look what I found." My parents would brag about my collection and my effort in front of the other children and I would feel so proud. This was a daily routine for years.

My mother was good at fixing things and repairing broken furniture. She made chairs out of orange crate boxes. Our clothes were made from material that flour and sugar came in. These ingredients were packed in flowery print fabric; not in paper like today. My mother would take a brown paper bag, place it on our body, trace our shapes, place it on the material and cut and sew perfectly fitting outfits. Croaker sacks were cut up and used as curtain and drapes for window coverings. Cooking was done on a black iron stove that burned wood. The wood had to be cut and placed in the stove to make the fire in order to cook. We carried water from a faucet by the lamp pole that came up out of the ground out by the road.

We had play clothes, school clothes and shoes, church clothes and shoes. The first thing you did when you came home from school was to change your clothes. On Saturday night was when we took a bath in a big tin tub in the kitchen, the water was heated on the stove. So you started early in the evening carrying buckets of water for filling into the tub. Other days we "washed- up" using a basin with water and soap that my mother made from lard and lye. We used baking soda to brush our teeth and for deodorant.

When I was fifteen, we moved out of "the woods" to Plainfield, New Jersey to a neighborhood that had just been integrated. An Italian family had just moved out of our house. Our family was the second colored family to move on that block. Our home at 534 West 5th Street was a two-story house.

It was the first time I had lived in a house with inside plumbing, hardwood floors, an ironing board that came out of the wall, venetian blinds, my own pillow and a double bed for my sister and me. We now had a room for the girls, a room for the boys, and a room for our parents. It was like a taste of Heaven on earth. Now, I was not ashamed to get a ride home from church.

My mother became ill and couldn't do certain things. I did the shopping for grocery. I always brought "the quick sells" items, using coupons. I always looked for the "Blue Light" special; only buying what was on sale or the buy one and get one free deals. I did this so my parents could brag on how much money I had saved the family. We had lived in the house less than two years when my father, on October 8, 1955, was killed in a car accident. Again, our style of living had to change.

I graduated from Plainfield High School on June 18, 1956 at the age of 18. I was still very active in the church. I had an electric IBM typewriter and an A.B. Dick memo graph machine set up in the cellar. I was responsible for copying the church bulletins.

I was married August 8, 1959 and moved to New Smyrna Beach, Florida. We lived in public housing. All three of my children were born while we were living in the projects. My experiences from my childhood were still with me, because I still had the same "follow the garbage truck" mentality – look for the sales, buy everything second-handed, and if you can't pay cash then you can't afford it.

My two sons had a paper route. I would drive them around as they threw the papers out of the back of a station wagon. Early in the morning, I would see the different piles of trash that were set out for the garbage man. I knew the pickup days for the rich neighborhoods. I would beat the garbage trucks and get anything I could use off the trash piles. Sometimes people would offer me things, just to have them removed. I used contact paper, paint, sanding to restore the furniture. I did what I saw my mother do, when I was growing-up. Many times our friends would marvel at the finished products. I was still following the garbage truck!

When I would purchase produce, I would always say to the clerk, "Would you mark this down because of this bruise or spot?" Of course, I always picked out soft or the fruit with blemish. When my daughter graduated from college she said, "Mama would you please promise me that you won't bring any more rotten fruit to this house and only buy Charmin toilet tissue? I want a chair that I am the first to sit in and a mattress that no one has slept on."

There was a time that my daughter and I went into a store to buy a mattress for my queen- size bed. I had shopped at this store before when my children were young and knew they sold used mattresses from hotels. The price for the new set of mattress and box springs was so high, that I started to have a panic attack. I insisted that they must have cheaper or used stuff. I embarrassed my daughter, but the clerk finally admitted that they did have some mix-matched mattresses and box springs in the rear of the store. I was so happy.

When I go into a store, I go right to the used or bargain area. Just the thought of paying full price for anything, makes me physically sick. When I need carpet, I first look in the outside bins at the carpet store. I was married for 35 years and I have been a widow for 20 years. Before my daughter recently moved me into a five bedroom, 3 ½-bathroom home with two living rooms, a formal dining room and large office, I never had a new car, stove, television, refrigerator, washing machine, dryer, or any type of new furniture – by choice. My daughter does not like used stuff, so I do not bring it into the new home. However, I get joy out of washing the throwaway paper plates and plastic forks, spoons and aluminum pans, so they can be used again.

I have reached the age seventy-five years, my strength; patience and eyesight are not what it used to be. Now if I find something on the roadside or trash pile, I'm not strong enough to pick it up and put in the car. My family refuses to help me because they feel that I do not have to use second or third hand stuff. We can now afford to pay the regular price for our needs and most of our wants. I must admit, I am tired of running after the garbage truck, but I do not know how to stop. Ii gives me pride to say, "Everything in my house is paid for."

I believe following the garbage truck is a learned behavior, but I don't know if this mentality can be reversed? Can one struggle so much until they're unable to receive God's blessing? Does one have to learn how to live on the "mountain top?" I question myself as to why I grieve when I'm given "name brand" or expensive things? I'm always trying to figure out how I can return the items and get many cheaper things. I enjoy wearing something that was used and given to me, more than I enjoy wearing a new item that I removed the tag from.

My children will shower me with nice things, but I feel so ungrateful and beg them not to spend their hard earned money on me. I have tried so hard to be thankful and receive their gifts with an appreciative spirit, but I can't hide my true feelings. It's so bad until they say among themselves, "Just give her money and let her do what she wants to with it." I enjoy giving, but am embarrassed with being given to. Yes, I know how to love and I make a strong effort to love everyone regardless of the cost. I do not need material things to feel loved. I love and live for my family and would like to please them. Many times I'll give in, but I also want to feel good within and make decisions and choices that all will satisfy everyone. My family refers to me as a "pack rat" because I save everything; even the gift wrapping paper, because I think someday I'll have need for it.

Once I was praising the Lord out loud for my many different pair of shoes and colors. I can remember when I only had two pairs of shoes which were black and white. My youngest daughter said, "I know you are not praising the Lord for plastic Payless Shoes." One time I was with all laughed, and one said, "I thought you were going to say air conditioning units."

Now my grandchild will drive me by a pile of items on the curbside, sometimes even stop and say, "Look Grand mama, there's a good dresser" or (whatever the item is) and then drive off laughing. In days past, I would go back and check those items out, but now I can't because I'm not strong enough to move it and bring it home. However, the item stays in my thoughts.

One day while listening to the radio, I heard a program called "The Swap Shop." I called and bid on a car for $25.00. I won and my husband used that car for years. One day while leading a funeral procession, our church members felt embarrassed and brought us a newer car. Our Deacon cut the old car down and used it for hauling for many more years.

Although, I want my days of running after the garbage truck to become "null and void", I remember how I read that to keep baby lambs from running away, sometimes a shepherd would have to break their legs and carry the lambs until they heal. To me, this means sometimes one has to "re-break" some bones or mentality, so they can mend correctly. Other times, it is dressing the wound and teaching people how to care for themselves. Much like a doctor wouldn't want to give a patient more crutches and pain medication as a final solution to a broken leg or problem; there is benefit in having the leg heal completely and used as God intended.

I know that God wants us to be fulfilled. According to John 10:10, He wants us to live an abundant life. If He created us, which He did, then He knows what makes us happy. He knows what we love to do. He knows because He built us this way, and He did it for a reason. I believe He has something so unique and amazing in mind for me that the lessons I've learn from this present life, as well as the one to come.

BLEST. BROKEN. GIVEN.

CHAPTER FOURTEEN

SALVATION IS AN INSIDE JOB: YOU MUST SERVE THE LORD FROM THE INSIDE OUT

I Corinthians 4:18 *states, "While we look not at the things which are seen, but at the things which are not seen; for the things which are seen are temporal, but the thing which are not seen are eternal."*

It is recorded in Ephesians 3:16, *"That he would grant you, according to the riches of his glory, to be strengthened with might by his spirit in the inner man; that Christ may dwell in your hearts by faith; that ye, being rooted and grounded in love."*

In order not to lose heart, as believers, we need to shift our focus from that which is seen, to that which is not seen, and from temporary problems, to the glorious rewards we will receive. The fruit of the Spirit are inward emotions and attitudes, such as: love, joy, peace, kindness, goodness, faithfulness, gentleness and self-control. Jesus said in St. John 7:38 *"He that believeth on me, as the scripture hath said, out of his belly (from his innermost) shall flow rivers of living water" The* first portion of I Samuel 16:**7** states… *"for the Lord seeth not as man seeth; for man looketh on the outward appearance, but the Lord looketh on the heart."*

Instead of looking at appearance, God searches the heart. It doesn't matter to the Lord, the style or color of our shoes or the length of our skirts. The state of our heart is far more significant than our physical appearance or natural ability. In our respective roles, it is imperative that we unite, on one accord in both mind and spirit as we endeavor to fulfill

God's Purpose as we serve Him from the inside out. God knows His plan and the working out of all things in accordance with His purpose. The Godly woman is responsible to study and proclaim His Revelation while awaiting its fulfillment. The assurance of fulfillment lies in God Himself and won't take any longer than God has planned.

Learning to serve the Lord from the inside out can be developing through our thoughts. The Holy Spirit visits us through our mind. Our thoughts can take us to the attic or to the cellar. Our thoughts determine our success or failure. Our thoughts control our strength or our weakness. Our thoughts can eliminate the inferiority complex created by a bad environment.

I Peter 3:3-4 states, *"Whose adorning let it not be that outward adorning of plaiting the hair, and of wearing of gold, or of putting on of apparel; but let it be the hidden man of the heart, in that which is not corruptible, even the ornament of a meek and quiet spirit, which is in the sight of God of great price."*

It is recorded in the Bible in Deuteronomy 22:5, *"The woman shall not wear that which pertaineth unto a man, neither shall a man put on a woman's garment: for all that do so are abomination unto the Lord they God."*

It is also recorded in I Timothy 2: 9-10 *"In like manner also, that women adorn themselves in modest apparel, with shamefacedness and sobriety; not with broided hair, or gold, or pearls, or costly array; but (which cometh women professing godliness) with good works."*

It is not ours to choose what to teach, what to eat or what to wear. The Word of God tells us exactly and precisely what those things are. The Word of God tells us exactly and precisely what these things should be. We are called to present our bodies as a living sacrifice, because we are not

100

our own; but are brought with a price. The woman of God is a chosen vessel of the Lord. She has been charged to take the plan of salvation to the masses and to provide a strong example of Apostolicism.

Beloved, we are to perpetuate the doings of the saints, like, in the beginning of the Church on the Day of Pentecost. We must maintain the highest standard of Apostolicism as described in the Word of God. It is our responsibility to promote the Apostolic Doctrine. We are built upon the foundation of the Apostles and Prophets, Jesus Christ Himself being the Chief Cornerstone.

Our mission is: "To **Evangelize**, the world for our Lord Jesus Christ, to **Equip** believers to become true Disciples of Christ; and to **Engage** those social problems that challenge the communities we are called to serve." (Mission Statement of COOLJC). Always remember the triple E's – Evangelize, Equip and Engage.

The Apostolic woman that lives by the Word is a support to her pastor and other leaders. She is a praying person and pays her tithes and offering and teaches her daughters to do the same. She studies the Word of God and hides it in her heart that she will not sin. She believes, teaches, and wholeheartedly supports the Word of God for the work of the ministry and the edifying of the Body of Christ.

It is recorded in I Corinthians 11th chapter, verses 4-15, *"Every man praying or prophesying, having his head covered, dishonoureth his head. But every woman that prayeth or prophesieth with her head uncovered dishonoureth her head; for that is even alone as if she were shaven.*

For if the woman be not covered, let her also be shorn: but if it be a shame for a woman to be shorn or shaven, let her be covered. For a man indeed ought not to cover his

101

head, forasmuch as he is the image and glory of God: but the woman is the glory of the man. For the man is not of the woman; but the woman of the man. Neither was the man created for the woman; but the woman for the man. For this cause ought the woman to have power on her head because of the angels. Nevertheless neither is the man without the woman, neither the woman without the man, in the Lord. For as the woman is of the man, even so is the man also by the woman; but all things of God. Judge in yourselves: is it comely that a woman pray unto God uncovered? Doth not even nature itself teach you, that, if a man has long hair, it is a shame unto him? But if a woman has long hair, it is a glory to her: for her hair is given her for a covering."

If we are to receive God's special blessing, then we must obey the Word and get to know and understand His will. He blesses obedience in ways we do not even think He will. Let it not be painful to us to accept God's Word. Rather, let us do it with joy. The Kingdom of God is inside of us. We don't need to seek outside for sources for God's joy, peace and love. Jesus left us the Holy Ghost that is everything we need to lead and guide us in the path of righteousness.

I Corinthians 6:19 states, *"What? Know ye not that your body is the temple of the Holy Ghost which is in you, which ye have of God, and ye are not your own? For ye are bought with a price: therefore glorify God in your body, and in your spirit, which are God's."*

Beloved, we need to examine our lives to find out to what extent we are willing to seek to know and follow the standards as the Lord has instructed us; remembering that His Grace is sufficient to enable us to walk upright before Him. God's grace speaks of the life long process of the Spirit filled believer who reconciles herself to sitting on the Potter's wheel so that God can mold and make her for His

102

Glory and Honor. The growth process is never appealing, but the results are extremely fruitful.

Isaiah 3:16-24 states *"Moreover the Lord saith, Because the daughters of Zion are haughty, and walk with stretched forth necks and wanton eyes, walking and mincing as they go, and making a tinkling with their feet: Therefore the Lord will smite with a scab the crown of the head of the daughters of Zion, and the Lord will discover their secret parts. In that day the Lord will take away the bravery of their tinkling ornaments about their feet, and their calf's, and their round tires like the moon. The chains, and the bracelets, and the mufflers, The bonnets, and the ornaments of the legs, and the headbands, and the tablets, and the earrings, The rings, and nose jewels, The changeable suits of apparel, and the mantles, and the wimples, and the crisping pins, The glasses, and the fine linen, and the hoods, and the veils. And it shall come to pass, that instead of sweet smell there shall be stink; and instead of a girdle a rent; and instead of well set hair baldness; and instead of a stomacher a girding of sackcloth; and burning instead of beauty.*

We commit the sin of omission when we do not obey the Word of God. Fashion and popularity are a poor price to pay for the loss of eternal life. Eternal life can be accomplished by doing the following:

- Studying the Word of God
- Expounding the Word of God
- Being patient one to another
- Having eyes for the blind
- Living peacefully and living Holy

The anointing comes from above, so we must look beyond man. Look to the Holy Spirit for guidance. When the Holy Spirit is able to operate freely within the Church of God, the Lord can be magnified and the believer's lights will shine from the inside out. We should not worry about dressing up the outside because there is no salvation in clothes. It is what comes out of a person that defiles or glorifies.

It is recorded in Matthew 15:11, 18 *"Not that which goeth in the mouth defileth a man; but that which cometh out of the mouth this defileth a man. But those things which proceed out of the mouth come forth from the heart; and they defile the man.*

Mark 7:15 states, *"There is nothing from without a man, that entering into him can defile him: but the things which come out of him, those are they that defile the man."*

We are living in a society where Satan is constantly trying to destroy the standard as described in the Word of God. Secular Humanism is encouraging us to *"be yourself,"* "do whatever you feel is right," without regard to the Scriptures. We must be about our Father's business; the Lord has called us unto holiness. *"For God hath not called unto uncleanness, but unto holiness"* is recorded in I Thessalonians 4:17. Jesus has called us unto glory and virtue and we must walk worth of the vocation wherein with we are called.

Every living being, even in the animal kingdom has to be in subjection to someone or something. God is a God of order. *"But I would have you know, that the head of every man is Christ; and the head of the woman is the man; and the head of Christ is God,"* is recorded in 1 Corinthians 11:3. This writer believes that it is urgently necessary that we uphold the standards addressed in the Word of God. We must remember that it is our responsibility to promote the Apostolic Doctrine.

When we make excuses for ourselves and for the people who do not a come up to the standards of the
104

Word of God, we sin by omission. This writing is an attempt to give Godly counsel in the fear of God, teaching those to walk shunning the very appearance of evil, that the Gospel be not blasphemed, because Salvation in an inside job and you must learn to serve the Lord from the inside so it will show on the outside.

"Woe unto you, scribes and Pharisees, hypocrites! For ye are like unto whited sepulchers, which indeed appear beautiful outward, but are within full of dead men's bones, and of all uncleanness. Even so ye also outwardly appear righteous unto men, but within ye are full of hypocrisy and iniquity" is recorded in Matthew 23:27, 28.

BLEST. BROKEN. GIVEN.

CHAPTER FIFTEEN

SEASONS OF A WOMAN'S LIFE

"While the earth remaineth, seedtime and harvest, and cold and heat, and summer and winter, and day and night shall not cease." –**Genesis 8:22, KJV**

This workshop will focus on the fact that *Seasons* are an integral part of God's program for the earth—and for women. That no woman is called to do all things at all times. This was recognized by the psalmists, the prophets and the apostles. Fruit comes in due season and so do tears (Psalm 1:3; 22:2). Rainy days come in seasons (Jer. 5:24; Ezek. 34:26). Prophetic words are fulfilled in their season (Luke 1:20). There are seasons of heaviness and seasons of rejoicing (I Pet. 1:6).

It seems that God, in His wisdom, punctuated all of life with seasons. Just as punctuation marks add meaning and variety to written communication, causing the reader to pause for understanding, accelerate with excitement or end abruptly at the conclusion, so seasons bring necessary meaning and variety to our lives.

The preacher in Ecclesiastes declares, *"To everything there is a season"* (Eccl. 3:1). In nature there is a progression from winter to spring to summer to fall. In our lives, too, there is a progression of change from one season to another. As surely as seasons direct the course of nature, so they direct the courses of our lives.

Understanding and accepting this can bring contentment. As Paul said, *"....For I have learned in whatever state I am, therewith to be content"* (Phil. 4:11). If we cooperate with the

Every season, from youth to old age, has its own responsibilities and rewards. Primary responsibilities change in various season, as they do, new opportunities become available. If we are sensitive to the varying responsibilities of each season, we can reap the reward of a greater harvest in seasons to come.

Changing Seasons or Stages in a Woman's Life

(I add the disclaimer that this is a generalization and that each woman is an individual and therefore ultimately subject to her own preferences).

The first season of Woman is SPRING (March to May) and relates to women from about 16 up to the age of 28 to 35. This is when she is exploring who she is and subject to the force of her age. The woman usually wants a mate to set up house with and to produce babies. In this season she may not have access to self- reflection and is often not fully aware of her own potential and her deep needs. Her instincts propel her to her fate, whether happy or challenging. Sixty-two percent of the females in the church are single.

The second season of Woman is SUMMER (June to August) which is from around thirty-six to fifty-five years. This is when a woman is starting to truly come into her own body and psyche. She starts to explore and acknowledge herself as a woman and therefore needs equality in her relationships with men. She is also happy for a man to worship her and at the very least to acknowledge her. Her identity does not hinge or depend on the man in her life as it would in SPRING Season of Woman. The relationship should just enhance who she is now.

The third season of Woman is FALL or AUTUMN (September to November) and this age is between fifty-six and seventy years of age for a woman. She is starting to notice changes and possible frailty in her body and commonly experiences the woes of menopause ('The Change' as it is often called). There can be challenges with her health during these years and there are definitely changes of focus or orientation. A woman can truly come into her inner-power this time. She knows her limits and her strengths much better now and she does not tolerate foolishness easily and likes to proceed directly from A to B. Life seems short now with no time to waste and she wants to fit as much in as she can. Quality is more important than quantity. So at this point she may need more independence from her man and definitely more respect as she flows into interesting life adventures. She may also like more mental challenge from her contact with men.

The average age of widowhood in the United States is fifty-six. As a result, half of all women over sixty-five live as widows. This high rate of widowhood occurs because women tend to marry men older than themselves. Also life expectancy for women is seven to nine years longer for women than for men.

The fourth season of Woman is WINTER (December to February) and is from around seventy-one or till the end of a woman's life. She has reached the three scores and ten that the Scripture promised her. This period of a woman's life is a coming home to her soul. She may not need anything from a man now and if she does it may just be his companionship and love as her partner. She is able to see all of who she is now; she is not burdened with the constrictions of hormonal changes that the last three seasons demand. She can enjoy herself, others, life and she can offer her valuable wisdom to others. She is like the finest wine and should be honored and sipped appropriately. She is more able to stand in her own right now than at any other time in her life. This is the time when she can enjoy the fruits of her life.

Ranking Priorities

If you have children at home, realize this: It is for only a short season! Responsibilities attended to well during the early years of motherhood can produce an extended harvest for the kingdom through the lives of your children. On the other hand, neglect during this season can produce wild tares and weeds for you to contend with in the seasons to come. With clear perspective, determine how much extended involvement you can manage, and do not feel guilty or repressed by your decision. Feel comfortable with the ranking order of your priorities, knowing that this season will pass and your present priorities will change.

My advice to all young mothers with a heart for ministry is this: Do what you can now. Plan and prepare for the future, but do not feel guilty and overload yourself during the formative years of your marriage and children. It is an important season with important priorities. Tend it well. Another season will come—and you will be prepared.

Women in Progress

Just as there are seasons in nature, in the physical body and in our life's work, there are also spiritual seasons. They are a part of the production process of the kingdom. Each one of us experiences times of *plowing, sowing and harvesting,* with all the attendant challenges and pleasures. The budding of a ministry with a fresh anointing is filled with expectancy. The blossoming time brings expectancy into recognition. The season of bearing fruit necessitates the work of preservation and sharing. Harvest is attended with great joy.

According to the law of production, fruit-bearing is rewarded with the repetition of the process. Our fruit becomes *more* fruit and progresses to the bounteous harvest of *much* fruit. It is important to remember, however, that a cycle of production is often preceded by a dormant season. This is a time during which it seems as if nothing is happening spiritually—when we feel stripped bare, buried in isolation, and forgotten. Such a time came to the Apostle John on the island of Patmos and to the Apostle Paul when he was in prison.

It may come to you in a time of sickness, loss, disappointment or rejection. I can assure you it will come— but only for a season! Be mindful that every bleak winter carries with it the promise of another spring. Whatever season you find yourself in, **practice patience,** and know that He who began the work in you is able to complete it (see Phil. 1:6). Patience is what keeps faith working. Refrain from judging yourself or others harshly in present circumstances.

But while a force beyond yourself determines your season, your reaction to the season is your responsibility. God determines when a particular season comes; your responsibility is to tend what has been planted. We would be foolish to try to plant in winter or harvest in spring. Yet we often resist the circumstances God has allowed to promote growth!

Stormy Weather

In every season, of course, storms may appear. You may be on a spiritual high when the ring of the telephone comes like a clap of thunder, bringing unexpected news of a calamity or loss. Even the best seasons of life can be clouded by a storm. At such times, thank God for the promises in His Word—that wonderful phrase of Scripture found 120 times with 120 verses, or 10 time for each month: *"It shall come to pass."* Storms come, and storms pass. They don't last forever. The sun will shine again!

The passing years and season, I've found, have galvanized my emotions. I know now that not every storm will sink my ship. (Hopefully, none of them will!) I also know that when the storm is raging, my feelings are not sure ground. I take heart in God's comments to Job—the man of many seasons, serial storms and bounteous blessings. There are treasures in the snow, God told Job, and hail is reserved for the days of trouble, wars, and battle. I have learned that today's tempest often will hold the sustenance and strength for the future. Storms can make channels for the rain, and tender new growth comes as result of the storm (see Job 38:22-23, 25-27).

Paul said we comfort others *"with the comfort with which we ourselves are comforted by God"* (II Cor. 1:4). The increasing fruitfulness of subsequent seasons, from which we nurture others, may often be augmented by the experience of a storm.

So whatever season of life you are in, make full use of it! Even a dormant season can become a special time for needed rest, quiet listening to God and fresh study. Don't waste time wishing you were someone else, somewhere else, doing something else. God made you as you are to use you as He planned. Living fully in your present is the best insurance for your future.

Understanding the law of seasons can relieve whatever pressure you feel about your current circumstances *and* increase your faith for the future. While we anticipate the fruit, we must understand the process: ***You will bring forth fruit in due season*** (see Psalm 1:13). Don't despair; the day of reaping will come!

In *due season,* we all have a reason to walk into our season, and it's okay to do it without fear. When we do, we learn how to *grow, develop,* and *maturate.* Yes, you will encounter spiritual warfare on the sojourn. Not to fear, but move steadfast to overcome, as you are challenged, while experiencing the "valley of life" encounters. I know we all *look* forward to that mountain top encounter. But it shall be the valley of life experience that will *refine, equip,* and *empower* you to meet the many obstacles and conflict that await you on the journey. We know that God may not always be early, but He is never late. The Comforter, though, is whenever He comes, He's always on time. All the blessings we yearn and thirst for; will come to us; when we learn to, "have faith" while we are walking into our season.

BLEST. BROKEN. GIVEN.

CHAPTER SIXTEEN

BLESSINGS CAN BE DELAYED, BUT NOT DENIED

"We are troubled on every side, yet not distressed; we are perplexed, but not in despair; Persecuted, but not forsaken; cast down, but not destroyed." II Corinthians 4:8, 9

AIM: The aim of this workshop is to show how Women of God must take Satan and demons seriously as they deal with their spiritual warfare. Spiritual warfare, simply put, is a struggle between good and evil. All believers face spiritual warfare. If you belong to Jesus, then you will engage in war against evil. We are in a spiritual warfare and we'll come out bloody and with scars. Jesus was wounded bruised, beaten and scourged for our example of suffering, and brokenness, for the salvation or wholeness of the world. Regardless of our tests, trials, rejections and tribulation, God expects us to live Holy. God's divine will is not always easy but it is always right.

OBJECTIVE: To show the Women of God the weapons for their battle is in prayer, Jesus and the Scripture. Spiritual warfare is dealing with three (3) key things the enemy sends at us: *temptations, deceptions* and *accusations.* God has secured the victory through Jesus Christ, but the Devil still has permission to attempt to wage war against God and His people, so that people can make a free will choice as to whom they will follow. God does this because He desires that none should perish but that all will have an opportunity to choose Him.

APPLICATION: To teach the Women of God that we are not victims when things goes wrong in our lives. This is the plan of the Lord and not the Devil, whom we give so much credit to, when we should be glorifying the Lord. Jeremiah 9:23-24 states, *"Thus saith the Lord, let not the wise man glory in his wisdom, neither let the mighty man glory in his might, let not the rich man glory in his riches:*

*But let him that glorieth, glory in this, that he **understandeth** and **knoweth me,** that I'm the Lord which exercise loving kindness, judgment, and righteousness, in the earth: For in these things I delight, saith the Lord."*

A **"Battle Cry"** is a yell or chant taken up in battle, usually by members of the same military unit. The content and nature of battle cries vary depending on whether their intent is to **threaten,** to give **courage, or** *to call on God for assistance.*

These cries can serve many purposes, including *"inspiring"* those otherwise inclined to stay back, *"terrifying"* the enemy as well as communicating to the allies that they have support.

A Battle Cry is aimed to invoke patriotic or religious sentiment, and their purpose is to arouse a feeling of pride in belonging to a group. The Battle Cry is designed to intimidate the enemy. It overstates one's own aggressive potential to a point where the enemy prefers to avoid confrontation all together and opts to flee. In order to overstate one's potential for aggression; "battle cries" need to be as loud as possible so that the enemy knows he does not stand a chance. The Biblical account of the Battle of Jericho in Joshua 6:1-27 has the "battle cry" of the

116

Israelites, amplified by horn-calls which collapsed the fortifications of the city under siege.

Today, the Battle Cry of the delegates in attendance at this Women's Council Retreat should be to call on the Lord for assistance and inform the Devil and all his demons under the sound of our voices that we, the women of God in this part of the vineyard, mean business and are on the battle field for the Lord.

Opening Prayer: *Lord, just as it is important for real soldiers to be ready for battle, it's important for us to be ready for the spiritual battle we are in with Satan. Our struggle is not against flesh and blood, but it is spiritual. You have given us "spiritual armor" to protect ourselves and to war successfully. Please give us good listening ears today so that we might not miss any of the instruction that You want to give us. In Jesus' name, we pray. Amen*

Please stand and examine yourself. Do you have on the correct helmet and sword? Ephesians 6:17 states, *"And take the helmet of salvation, and the sword of the Spirit, which is the Word of God."* The sword is an offensive weapon and is meant to tear down and kill the enemy's troops. Let's take up the sword of the Spirit (God's Word) today, and start slaughtering the enemy's assets that he's been using against us.

Is your abdomen wrapped with the belt of truth? The belt of truth protects the soldier's vital organs and held the other pieces of the armor in place. You use the belt of truth (God's Word) to guard against the enemy's deception (lies) that he sends your way, while you use the sword of the Spirit (also God's Word) to tear down strongholds (deception that took hold) in your mind. John 7:38-*39 "He that believeth on Me, as the scripture hath said, out of his belly shall flow rivers of living water'.* (But this spake He of the Spirit, which they that believe on Him should receive: for the Holy Ghost was not yet given; because that Jesus was not yet glorified). How can the women of God put on the belt of truth? There are two ways. First, by learning as much as we can of the Bible's truths, and second, by always being truthful in everything we do.

We have two weapons to deal with deceptions: the belt of truth (Ephesians 6:14) and the sword of the Spirit (Ephesians 6:17) which is the Word of God. Both are truths, which are found in God's Word, so why are they given two different names (a sword and a belt?). Because one is meant to be defensive (the belt), while the other is meant to be offensive (the sword). A belt is something you wear to guard against an attack, while a sword is used to slaughter the enemy.

Do you have on your Satan-proof vest? It is the breastplate of righteousness! Not our righteousness obviously, but the righteousness of God through Christ Jesus. Our righteousness is as filthy rags (Isaiah 64:6), but because of the work of the cross, we can receive the righteousness of God through Christ Jesus (Romans 3:22, Galatians 3:6). Therefore when the enemy tries to remind us of our past, tell him it's been washed away (II Corinthians 5:17), our sins have been forgotten (Hebrews 10:17) and we have the righteousness of God (Romans 3:22).

What about your shoes? Do you have the correct shoe on the one prepare for the Gospel of Peace? The Scripture calls the believer's shoes, "the preparation of the gospel of peace." What does this mean? Well, the word "gospel" means "good news." So the Scripture is calling these shoes "the preparation of the good news of peace." Basically, this saying, "be prepared to tell people the good news about the peace we have with God."

If anyone asked you what the gospel is, could you tell them? Well, the gospel is the good news that Jesus died for our sins—our sins are forgiven. The whole gospel story is that Jesus was born; He died for us; He arose; now He's in Heaven with His father, but He is coming back again.

The way to put on your gospel of peace shoes is to believe Jesus really did pay the penalty for your sins. We can also do this by making peace with others. We have peace with others by being kind to them, forgiving them (Ephesians 4:32), and doing our best to build them up, not tear them down (Ephesians 4:29). Remember women of God, when Mary did not help Martha her sister, Martha did not "attack" her sister or tear her down. She just told Jesus and He worked it out. Don't wrestle with your sister – tell it to Jesus!

Watch your feet! Be sure you are wearing your gospel of peace shoes. You will need them so you will be prepared to tell people the good news about Jesus. If you are prepared to share the Gospel with people, then you will be able to stand firm against Satan.

The most important piece of equipment is the shield of faith. It allows you to stop the fiery darts of Satan and all his imps. The fiery darts of the enemy are accusations sent our way. For example, when the Devil tries to accuse us of our past sins, we are to have faith in the work of the cross and know that we are forgiven and not to look back. The Lord has given us goodness and mercy to protect our backs.

Our battle cry will be coming from Psalms 24: verses 7-10. Let us now march in time, and follow my instructions, answering my questions under one voice.

Lift up your heads, O ye gates; and be ye lift up, ye everlasting doors; and the King of glory shall come in.
Who is this King of glory?

(Audience: The Lord strong and mighty, the Lord mighty in battle.)

Lift up your heads, O ye gates; even lift them up, ye everlasting doors; and the King of glory shall come in.

Who is this King of glory?

(Audience: The Lord of hosts, He is the King of Glory.)

FORWARD ALWAYS –
BACKWARD NEVER!

Sing:

Victory ahead! Victory ahead!
Through the blood of
Jesus, Victory ahead;
Trusting in the Lord, I
hear the Conqueror's
tread, By faith I see the
Victory ahead!

(Please take your seat)

IWC Theme Song, *"Victory Ahead"* which was written by William Grum in 1905, based on I John 5:4-5 *"For whatsoever is born of God overcometh the world: and this is the victory that overcometh the world, even our faith. Who is he that overcometh the world, but he that believeth that Jesus is the Son of God?"*

Victory Ahead

"When the hosts of Israel, led by God, Round the walls of Jericho softly trod, Trusting in the Lord, they felt the conqueror's tread, by faith they saw the victory ahead.

David with a shepherd's sling and five stones, Met the giant on the field all alone, Trusting in the Lord, he knew what God had said, By faith he saw the victory ahead.

121

Daniel prayed unto the Lord thrice each day,
Then unto the lion's den led the way, Trusting in
the Lord, he did not fear or dread, By faith he
saw the victory ahead.

Often with the carnal mind I was tried,
Asking for deliverance oft I cried, Trusting
in the Lord, I reckoned I was dead, By faith
I saw the victory ahead.

When like those who've gone before to that land, By
death's river cold and dark I shall stand; Trusting in the
Lord, I will not fear or dread, By faith I see the victory
ahead."

These words are recorded in II Corinthians 4:8, 9, 10 verses (KJV) *"We are troubled on every side, yet not distressed; we are perplexed, but not in despair; Persecuted, but not forsaken; cast down, but not destroyed; Always bearing about in the body the dying of the Lord Jesus, that the life also of Jesus might be made manifest in our body."* We suffer persecution but are not forsaken; we are cast down, but we perish not, persecuted, but not abandoned, cast down, but not destroyed!

Apostle Paul spoke these words to the Church at Corinth, the Corinthians, who were believers. As believers, we will face trials. But we must remember, women of God, that God controls trials and uses them to strengthen us. However, Paul's main purpose for writing Second Corinthians was to defend his ministry. He wrote this letter to prove that his ministry was sincere and genuine, and to reassert his authority as an Apostle of Christ. Paul was not forsaken by the Lord but he was struck down. But he was not destroyed, that is, killed. The Lord spared his life so that he could continue to preach the Good News, the Gospel, the death, burial, and resurrection of our Lord and Savior Jesus Christ.

The thought that I want you to meditate on for a few minutes is: **YOUR BLESSINGS CAN BE DELAYED, BUT NOT DENIED!!** Our current day application is that God always keeps His promises!! God can reverse a situation to accomplish His will!! The believers should never give up on God. He may not come when you want Him but He is always on time!!

The first command found in the Bible given to the human race was: ***"Be fruitful and multiply"*** (Genesis 1:28). Male and female were given the responsibility of filling the earth. God blessed them, bestow His favor upon them with the commandment and promise to be fruitful. Yet, it is interesting to note that so many of the leading women in the Bible were barren, not able to reproduce; not capable of bearing children. According to the Scriptures, in the first book, Genesis, Sarai was the first who experienced a period of infertility. Others who followed were Rachel, Leah, Rebecca, Samson's mother (Manoah's wife), the Shumanite woman, Hannah and Elizabeth of the New Testament.

In the Eastern culture, having many children was a sign of a Divine blessing. In Old Testament times, a woman who was childless was considered to be cursed by God. When a woman was not able to conceive a child, her husband could divorce her. Childless widows usually returned to their parents' home. It was through the line of Abraham and Isaac that God was going to send the

Redeemer. If there were no children, the line of descendants would stop. Some things seem to take a long time to happen, but that does not mean they will not take place, for example, in the fullness of time, God gave His Son to the earth. The women who were once barren later had children. **DELAYED, BUT NOT DENIED!!** Some remained faithful to God through the pain (as did Elizabeth); others used other methods (as did Sarai) to obtain children—methods that led only to sorrow.

After a period of barrenness, the Lord specifically gave a child in the line of promise. Each of these Biblical women prayed and waited upon the Lord. In due time, God responded to their prayers. The more familiar we become with how God worked in the past, the better equipped we are for learning His will for the present and the future. To the potential mothers under the sound of my voice, you must realize that the conception or lack of conception of children is the hands of the Sovereign God.

In Genesis 16:1, 2 The Scriptures declare, *"Now Sarai Abram's wife bare him no children: and she had no children: and she had a handmaid, an Egyptian, whose name was Hagar. And Sarai said unto Abram, Behold now, the Lord hath restrainth me from bearing: I pray thee, go in unto my maid; it may be that I may obtain children by her. And Abram hearkened to the voice of Sarai. But in Genesis 21:2 you will find these words, "For Sarah conceived, and bare Abraham a son in his old age, at the set time of which God had spoken"* **DELAYED BUT NOT DENIED!!**

Then there is the story of two sisters Leah and Rachel. It is recorded in Genesis 29:31 "*And when the Lord saw that Leah was hated, He opened her womb: but Rachel was barren.*" The Scripture goes on to say in Genesis 30: 22-23, "*And God remembered Rachel, and God hearkened to her, and opened her womb, and she conceived, and bares a son: and said, God hath taken away my reproach.*" After Leah had four sons for Jacob, she stops bearing but the Lord harkened unto Leah and she conceived and bore Jacob two more sons and a daughter.

Jacob's twelve sons, the tribes of Israel, came through six sons from Leah, two sons from Rachael (Joseph and Benjamin) two sons from Bilhah (Rachel's maid), and two sons from Zilpah (Leah's maid). Leah's fourth son was Judah, the tribe that our Lord and Savior came from.

Then you will read in Genesis 25:21 "*And Isaac entreated the Lord for his wife, because she was barren: and the Lord was entreated of him, and Rebekah his wife conceived.*" Sarah, Leah, Rachel and Rebekah four barren woman found in the book of Genesis.

Another example of barren women in the Bible can be seen relative to the Shunamite woman. In II Kings 4:14 "*And he said, what then is to be done for her? And Gehazi answered, verily she hath no child, and her husband is old.*" "*Then the woman conceived, and bore a son at that season that Elisha had said unto her, according to the time of life*" (II Kings 4:17).

Biblical barrenness is also found in the Book of I Samuel 1:2 *"And he had two wives; the name of the one was Hannah, and the name of the other Peninnah: and Peninnah had children, but Hannah had no children."* But in I Samuel I: 20 *you read* these words *"Wherefore it came to pass, when the time was come after Hannah had conceived, that she bare a son, and called his name Samuel, saying, because I have asked him of the Lord."*

Hannah, one of the wives of Elkanah, a Levite, bore great sorrow because of her barrenness. Having no children might not have been so bad if she had not been provoked by her husband's other wife Peninnah. Peninnah fruitfulness lifted her to a level of haughtiness while Hannah's barrenness caused her to be discontent and harbor sorrow in her heart. The barrenness of Hannah was not on her part. The Lord had shut up her womb. *Many times, the Lord keeps our immediate desires from us because He has something greater for us in the future.*

Elkanah was aware of the unrest in his family and thought by chance that the trip to Shiloh where they could worship together would command the attention of both. However the situation seemed to grow worst because Peninnah kept up her harassment. *Women of God, our adversaries reap joy when we show evidence of grief and a sorrowing spirit.* Hannah was encouraged to keep her spirit in spite of the harassment from Peninnah.

The sorrow that enveloped Hannah took her appetite and affected her attitude. However, her husband loved her in spite of her barrenness and continued to encourage her spirit. Women of God, Christ has **"an in spit e of love "** for

His church regardless of our infirmities and faults.

Hannah's sorrow drove her to make a special appeal to the Lord. Her cry was a plea to be remembered and be granted a child that she would later give back to the Lord. She was rebuked but was also granted her request. *Whenever we come to the Lord with problems, He is able to change the situation or give us comfort in the midst of difficulty.*

Women of God, remember that our sorrow must never cause us so much despair that we fail to remember the mercies and goodness of God and let it affect our attitude of worship.

Elizabeth represents another Biblical example of a barren woman who was forced to completely place her trust in God of her salvation. Luke 1:7 *"And they had no child, because that Elizabeth was barren, and they both were now well stricken in years."* Then in Luke 1:24 you'll read *"And after those days his wife Elizabeth conceived, and hid herself for five months."* Without God's blessing, nothing and no one can flourish. Only the all-powerful God can create living things that can reproduce. **DELAYED, BUT NOT DENIED**

Women of God from each of these examples of a barren woman, the believer is reminded that, God always, provides. Although He gives us what we need, it may not be what we want. God always has a plan, but He does not always explain it to us in advance as He did to Rebekah. When Rebekah was barren, she pleaded for a child to avoid embarrassment and shame. She had a difficult pregnancy and sought the Lord about it. She was told that two nations were in her womb.

Certainly, the Lord is a covenant-keeping God and He will do the impossible for all who trusts Him. God is also a promise keeper. Whatever He promises us, we can expect it!! We must be aware of what God has promised to be and to do. Having children was intended to be the instrument used to establish the Kingdom of God so that the good news may be passed from generation to generation.

Through prayer we receive answers, instructions, comfort and strength to contend for the faith that was once delivered unto the saints. Certainly **prayer** is the catalyst that will enable us to press toward the mark of the high calling in Christ Jesus. Just what is **prayer? Prayer** is direct communication with God. **Prayer** is enjoying the presence of God. Every born again believer must establish and maintain a good relationship with God. That relationship can only be accomplished through **prayer.**

I believe those barren women knew what their purpose was to be fruitful and multiply. Whatever it took to accomplish this mission to replenish the earth they would dedicate ever decision and action toward achieving that purpose. Real meaning and significance comes from understanding and fulfilling God's purposes for putting us on earth. If it takes eavesdropping as Sarah did, or hatred and anger like Rachel; one must always be determined for God's Divine Will to be fulfilled, **not** His permissive will. Perhaps one will have to make a vow like Hannah, or you may have look out for the man of God like the Shunamite woman. Regardless of the task, the believer must completely trust the Lord. The task may be challenging. For example, one may have an unbelieving husband like Elizabeth. Whatever it takes, we must hold on to God's promises and He will fulfill the incredible plan for our lives.

Women of God, let us always remember the starting place must be with God and His eternal purpose for each life. Only the all-powerful God can create living things that can reproduce. One can trust a God whose decrees will always come to be. Don't take childbearing for granted. Remember it is a God-given privilege to be a responsible partner with Him in His work.

The first very promise of a Redeemer was given to Adam and Eve in Genesis 3:15. *"And I will put enmity between thee and the woman, and between thy seed and her seed; it shall bruise thy head, and thou shalt bruise his heel."* But it would be through Abraham's line that the Messiah would come to the earth. Women of God, remember "our heel" is the first thing that goes down, as we walk, with Christ.

"God created man in His own image, in the image of God created he him; male and female created He them:" (Genesis 1:27). God made the first man and woman in His likeness. God made us with three parts: body, soul, and spirit. God gave us bodies to live on the earth. Our bodies are not like God, because God does not live in a body. However, our Creator gave us a soul and a spirit. The soul is that part of us that responds not just to our environment but has a longing for even greater things. The spirit is like God. Our souls and spirits are eternal. Our bodies may decay, but the soul and spirit part of us will live forever. In this way, we are in God's image. Humans are the only creation God made on earth that can have fellowship with Him. God's faithfulness is evident in spite of human error. God is not dependent on us, but He has chosen to use us, even when some times our blessings feel delayed, they are not denied.

In my conclusion, the birth of Isaac was a blessing to Abraham and Sarah and a sign that succeeding families would realize that the Hebrew race began with a baby from a once barren woman. Our Christian faith began with a miracle baby, Jesus Christ, from a virgin, who took on human form so that He could redeem us. I believe barrenness was used because the children of Israel did evil things over and over again in the sight of the Lord. Rebellion caused the Lord to constantly have to deliver them out of trouble.

He had to prepare something special to help with the process. All of the children born from once barren women did great things:

- The birth of a previously barren woman nearly one hundred years old, who was laughing at the thought of having a child, was a miraculous event- Sarah and Isaac.

- The womb of Manoah's barren wife was opened and she gave birth to Samson, who was to turn a lion inside out, kill a thousand men, and pull down a pagan temple.

- The birth of Samuel, the prophet and anointer of the Kings, to the barren Hannah, whose womb the Lord had shut, revealed divine providential power.

- Elizabeth was barren, but through the power of God she gave birth to John the Baptist, of whom Jesus said there had yet been no one greater." (Matthew 11:11)

THANK GOD FOR BARRENNESS!!! OUR BLESSINGS CAN BE DELAYED, BUT NOT DENIED BECAUSE OF HIS PROMISES!!!

Women of God, always remember when we feel that situations are tough and that no one cares, we can always look to the Lord, knowing that He delights in doing things that seem to be impossible.

BLEST. BROKEN. GIVEN.

CHAPTER SEVENTEEN

VISION OF A DEPARTMENT OF THE WOMEN'S MINISTRIES OF THE CHURCH OF OUR LORD JESUS CHRIST OF THE APOSTOLIC FAITH, INC.

"Where there is no vision, the people perish: but he that keepeth the law, happy is he."
Proverbs 29:18

MISSION STATEMENT

The Mission of the Women's Ministries of the Church of Our Lord Jesus Christ of the Apostolic Faith, Incorporated is to engage, to empower and equip women for the up building of the Kingdom of God, to serve as godly examples in their home, communities and the world.

LEADERSHIP

The **Apostolic Mother** is the leader (President) of the Department of Women's Ministries of the Church of Our Lord Jesus Christ of the Apostolic Faith, Incorporated. She is the liaison between the Women's Department and the Board of Apostles for women's concerns.

She is recommended to the Board of Apostles by the Presiding Apostle of COOLJC. Upon his recommendation, the Board of Apostles will receive her for instruction and testing by the National Catechism Committee. After successful completion of testing she will receive her official appointment.

Her direction for the Women's Ministries will come from the Apostle to the Women. She must believe, practice and support the doctrine and vision of the COOLJC.

She must be dedicated, loyal and a consecrated senior Mother, with at least fifty (50) years of service to COOLJC.

She must have served as a past President of an International Women's Auxiliaries.

She should have at least four (4) years of Religious Studies from an institution of higher learning.

She must be willing to dedicate her talent, give of her time, resources and influences to study, teach and spread the Gospel at home and abroad. She must encourage the women of COOLJC to do the same.

She must have administrative abilities, be compassionate, congenial and have a sincere desire to promote the vision of the COOLJC. She must strive to always maintain the trust and confidentiality that is needed to work with the leaders of the organization. A strong, well- organized, women's department should be her goal.

The **Apostolic Mother**, under the direction of the Apostle to the Women, is then empowered to:

> Appoint her official staff and personnel to assist her in carrying out the program for the women's ministry of the COOLJC. The officers of this

Department shall consist of three (3) Vice-President, of the Missionaries, the International Women's Council and the Ministers' and Deacons' Wives' Guild, Recording Secretary, Corresponding Secretary, Financial Secretary, Treasurer and Chaplain.

- Conduct workshops with spiritual training, regardless of age, credential as well as non-credential holding for all females. The major work of the Department of Women's Ministries (DWM) is mission action, missionary education and evangelism.

- Implement financial obligations to raise at least $25,000 each annually for Education (W. L. Bonner College of Columbia, SC and the Christ Bible Institute, NY), Evangelism,

- Global and Home Mission Departments of COOLJC, $100,000 or more when possible.

- She or her designee will report all finance from the women's auxiliaries to the Executive Secretary Office within thirty (30) days after the close of the meeting.

- A full financial accounting of all income and expenditures should be submitted to the Apostle to the Women.

  - The Apostolic Mother greatest concern should be the up building of the Kingdom of God.

    Her focus should be on instructing women to build ministries through prayer and evangelism.

  - The Department of Women's Ministries is mandated to carry out the work of the Lord as stipulated by the parent body. It makes no laws; it follows the law of order of the COOLJC Apostles Board.

THE DEPARTMENT OF WOMEN'S MINISTRIES (DWM) IS COMPRISED OF THE FOLLOWING AUXILIARIES:

- The Department of Women's Missionary Work of Church of Our Lord Jesus Christ of the Apostolic Faith, Inc. Organized September 8, 1923, by the Executive Board of the National Convocation of the Church of Our Lord Jesus Christ, New York City, N.Y.

- The International Women's Council Church of Our Lord Jesus Christ of the Apostolic Faith, Inc. (Ratification Pending).   Have convened each October since 1952

- The International Ministers' and Deacons' Wives' Guild of the Church of Our Lord Jesus Christ of the Apostolic Faith, Inc. Duly ratified and accepted at the 53rd National Convocation of the Church of Our Lord Jesus Christ of the Apostolic Faith, Inc., August 1972.

ANNUAL SESSION MEETINGS

The Department of the Women's Ministries will meet on Wednesday, Thursday and Friday, after the third Sunday in October each year, at a pre-designated place. Wednesday the Missionaries will preside, Thursday the International Women's Council will be in charge and close out on Friday with the Ministers' and Deacons'

Wives' Guild. A planning/business session will convened at the annual Seminar for each of these ministries.

TENURE AND DUTIES OF OFFICERS

Officers serve a three-year term, limited to a two-term tenure of office (a maximum of six years).

PRESIDENT (The Apostolic Mother): Shall preside over all meetings, and be responsible for all the general business of the Department of the Women's Ministries (DWM). Be fully committed to fulfill the cause of Christ. To give nourishment, encouragement and Spiritual enrichment to the women of COOLJC.

VICE-PRESIDENT: Shall assist the President in all of her duties. The duty of the Vice- President over the Missionaries is to designed, enhance and advance the qualities of the women of COOLJC which are imperative for a Christ centered life. To train them to do their part in harvesting souls for Jesus Christ and to labor together with the brethren in establishing churches and spreading the truth. The Missionaries will target the **seasoned women** with an evangelism overtone. An offering for **Evangelism** will be raised during the Night Service.

The duty of the Vice-President over the Women's Council is that since all females who are members of any legally constituted local church in COOLJC are automatically member of this organization, should help members of all ages, gain knowledge and deal with issues which relate to women and society. To help females grow in grace and in the knowledge of our Lord Jesus Christ and to support the financial goals of COOLJC. The Women's Council will target the **0-40 age group, single, separated, divorce** with the family overtones. An offering for **Education** will be raised during this Night Service.

The duty of the Vice-President over the Ministers' and Deacons' Wives' Guild is to equip and prepare women to establish a team relationship with their husbands and to form a partnership that will magnify and glorify the Lord, therefore, encouraging and winning lost souls for Christ. The Guild will address the psychological needs of women and be a support group, to the wives of ministers and deacons. The Ministers' and Deacons' Wives' Guild will target the **Widows and Wives of the Apostles, Bishops and Deacons.** An offering for **Global and Home Mission** will be raised during the Night Service.

RECORDING SECRETARY: Shall keep record of all proceedings at all regular and special meetings. Shall keep record and attend to the filing of all committee reports. Prepare the minutes for publishing in the Minute Book for the Executive Staff of COOLJC.

CORRESPONDING SECRETARY: Shall keep record of the names and addresses of all International Officers, all State and Local President, all Committee Chairperson, and registered delegates. Shall attend to all official correspondence and communication, and send to all local Presidents and State Presidents all pertinent information concerning meetings. She is automatically a member of the Registration Committee.

FINANCIAL SECRETARY: Shall keep record of all incomes to the DWM from any source. Shall keep record of all requests for expenditures and/or appropriations. Shall prepare a computer spread sheet report and submit to the President on request of all funds received and/or disbursed since the previous Council. Shall automatically serves as Chairman of the Finance Committee.

TREASURER: She deposits the funds of the DWM. Shall keep an accurate record of all deposits and withdrawals and/or checks written, and shall submit a written report of same at the DWM meetings, or to the President on request.

CHAPLAIN: Shall conduct devotional services at all regular DWM meetings, along with representatives of different States.

BLEST. BROKEN. GIVEN.

CHAPTER EIGHTEEN

BRUISED, BUT DELIVERED AND PERSUADED TO CONTINUE THE VISION

"Though he slay me, yet will I trust in him: but I will maintain mine own ways before him."
Job 13:15

Secular tradition often depicts Friday the 13th as a day characterized by bad luck and misfortunes. Yet, twelve years ago in Denver, Colorado; Friday 13, 2000, proved to be a blessed day of a new beginning for me. It was a day that has forever changed my life. I vividly recall the power of the Lord overtaking me as I received the prophetic pronouncement of being named the ninth President of the International Women's Council of the Church of Our Lord Jesus Christ of the Apostolic Faith, Inc. The International Women's Council is the only women auxiliary in COOLJC in which membership is not exclusive. Any adult female member in good standing with a local church within the Church of Our Lord Jesus Christ is a member of the International Women's Council. The Council is composed of over 30,000 members in the United States of America and five different countries.

My heart pounded and a confidence I'd never before witnessed rested within my bosom, as my life-long dream became a reality. Before I traveled to Denver, I had no idea this would happen. However, I was fully confident, that the Hand of the Lord was laid upon me on that night.

I spent the next three years, discovering ways of totally surrendering myself, my family and my resources to the Will of the Lord while leading the women of this great organization. The Scripture declares, *for ye are brought with a price, therefore glorify God in your body, and in your spirit, which are God's"* (I Corinthians 6:20). Though I was familiar with this passage, the Lord led me on a journey that caused me to live it like never before. I truly became the God- ordained spiritual property of the International Women's Council (IWC) and the Church of Our Lord Jesus Christ (COOLJC). From the early morning until the late in the night, the telephone would ring without end. The mailbox, fax machine and e-mails would find me wherever I was, regardless of what I was doing. The intensity was so strong, the only way to survive was to prayerfully yield to the will and direction of the Lord. In doing so Jesus daily granted me favor with both God and man (Luke 2:52).

I was like a little rosebud that the Lord ordained to blossom for the appointed time. Having grown up with a severe speech impediment, I suddenly found myself addressing audiences of thousands and not reaching for a single word. The lifelong quietness had prepared me to listen to the voice of the Almighty God.

He worked on me and through me like never before. My travel itinerary remained full. The Lord spoke to me telling me to remain approachable and down to earth. He told me to be a Mother who not only loves her children, but someone that the people would want to love. The love I received cannot be denied. They put their arms around me and placed their trust in me. I stayed in their homes, and kept myself accessible and available to minister to the needs of such a diverse group of Holy women and daughters. God blessed exceedingly, abundantly; above all I could ask or think. Every high place was brought down; every expectation was exceeded beyond measure.

I received the gift of the Holy Ghost at the age of nine. I was saved on June 18, 1947 in Scotch Plains, New Jersey and was the first young person saved under the ministry of the late Bishop Robert S. Grayer. My love for the IWC was instilled within me when I was a child. I grew up working diligently in the Garden State. I graduated from Plainfield High School in 1956. I saved the money that I received from the church and my family and used it to attend the IWC in Bluefield, West Virginia that year. My soul and spirit were overwhelmed with what I saw and felt. Then I petitioned, "Lord, would you please one day let me wear the cape in which the IWC President, Mother Perry was draped." I began serving in the Council then since October of 1956.

I've worked locally, State, District and Diocese at all levels in different capacity. I've traveled throughout the United States and have visited five of the seven continents, twice while attending an IWC held on the foreign field. I've worked the registration desk, served on various committees, served as a District and Diocese Women's Council President, International Vice- President of Education for four years and then became the International President. Presently, I am Region Ten Director of the Women's Department.

God bestowed these experiences upon me. No one or nothing can erase these precious memories. I'm fully persuaded, therefore, to complete the vision that was started by our founder, Mother Delphia Perry and passed down through the years. As an observant teenager, I admired Mother Perry's tams (hats) and her cape. To me, they were symbols of modesty and motherhood. Having experienced the blessed opportunity to sit in her seat, the most sought after seat in COOLJC, I now realize her garment were clothes fit for a soldier. There's a great price to pay in order to wear these apparel. The costs and benefits were equally overwhelming.

I thank God for record-breaking success in numerous categories. The three-year *record*, including the overall number of souls saved and baptized, as well as, the

143

presence of 260 first- time attendees at our meeting of October 2003. As recorded in Hebrew 6:10 *"For God is not unrighteous to forget your work and labor of love, which ye have shown toward His name in that ye have ministered to the saints and do minister.*

Prior to the 2003 meeting, I shared with my family a recurring dream God had given me. In this dream, I saw hundreds of souls coming to the altar. (I now believe that this was the 260 first-time attendees that came forth). I told my family these people that came forth in the dream were not coming to be baptized, but they were already spirit-filled. I also saw myself walking hand in hand with Bishop Bonner. As he would stop, kiss, and embrace the different sisters, I said to myself, "What should I do?" So I started to kiss and embrace. That's why I now feel that I should follow the legacy of Bishop Bonner in genuinely embracing and loving people, all people. Unity was not simply an administrative slogan. It's my heart's conviction. That's why I am persuaded even more now than ever to continue the vision. Unity is my theme and Glory is my goal.

Whoever coined the phrase, "sticks and stones can break your bones but names cannot hurt you," was wrong! I heard words over nine years ago, and they still hurt. Yes, the wounds have healed but the scars are still with me. I thank the Lord for having taken me through the fire and bringing me out blessed and not bitter. The initial shock from the process in which the change occurred was quite distressing. Yet, the Lord reminds me to live the Scripture that I have so often quoted, "Lift up your heads, Oh ye gates....Yes, the King of Glory stepped in.

In spite of the surveys completed by the women of God expressing extreme satisfaction, the financial record of increased revenue, the unprecedented attendance records, the number of souls saved, my constant reporting to him and the Board of Apostles in regularly scheduled cabinet meetings with positive feedback from them, etc., the Presider came into my room on the final night of a successful convention and said, "The women of the Church of Our Lord are not where I think they should be and under your administration I don't think they will get where I desire them to be... So, I feel that I must make a change and not reinstate you as president for the next three years." He went on to say, "There is an undercurrent of suppressed women that is not bold enough to tell you this to your face."

Those words hit me, through and through and it was like being struck with a bolt of lightning. I was devastated! Words also reviled me. When I questioned the Chief Apostle of COOLJC about this decision, he stated that he did not have any executive authority on decision making of the Board of Apostles but "Out of all the women that sat in that seat, you came the closest one to being an Apostolic Mother."

Beloved, believe me, I've been commanded to present my body as a living sacrifice. I'm not my own. I've been brought with a price. I believe that it was urgently necessary that I uphold the standards of Apostolicism. I felt it was my responsibility to promote the Apostolic Doctrine, by doing what the Apostles did. We are built upon the foundation of the Apostles and Prophets, Jesus Christ Himself being the Chief Cornerstone.

The Apostolic Doctrine must be conformed to as it relates to women and their ministry in the Church, the Body of Christ. The Church of Our Lord Jesus Christ has been a model for the rest of the Pentecostal world as it relates to the proper place of women in the ministry. This organization is a continuation of the original Church founded on the Day of Pentecost and it is important that we maintain the highest standard of Apostolicism as described in the Word of God. We are living in a society where traditional family values are under attack.

I would like to remind you of the importance of cherishing our Apostolic Heritage. The Church of Our Lord Jesus Christ is a chosen vessel of the Lord. The Lord has charged us to take the plan of salvation to the masses and to provide a strong example of Apostolicism. The Lord Jesus Christ has used this organization to impact millions of women all over the world.

I felt blessed before the title of President of the International Women's Council of the Church of Our Lord Jesus Christ was conferred on me. I had favor with God and man. I am a chosen vessel. This position was just an office that I desired to serve in, which I felt was a good thing.

I now believe my removal, after I had served three years, was ordained by God. When I was first appointed to this position, the Lord spoke to me and said, "Get your head out of the cloud and follow the cloud." Because I had been dreaming and practicing for so many years I thought it meant, you can stop day dreaming, now and get down to the business at hand. However, I realize now that the Lord was telling me to face reality. Look earthly and see what you're surrounded with; but keep your eyes on me, you're in the earth but not of the earth.

The Scriptures that brought comfort and peace of mind to me were Hebrew 6:10 and Romans 8:28, *"For God is not unrighteous to forget your work and labor of love, which ye have shewed toward His name, in that ye have ministered to the saints, and do minister." "And we know that all things work together for good to them that love God, to them who are the called according to His purpose."*

I am remembering God's charge of nurturing and mothering to me and the Scripture *"Let the aged woman teach the younger women"* and *"Teach your daughters wailing."* I realize now and accept the fact that my work in

146

that part of the vineyard was completed. I've responded to the voice of the Lord. I believe I've fought a good fight, I've kept the faith and I will graciously close this course of my life with complete gratitude and gratefulness.

I will continue to Mother and love, just as the Lord has instructed me to do. Yes, I'm bruised with scars, but I'm delivered and persuaded to continue the vision that was passed down to me. I will always remember whose seat I'm sitting in. I don't feel that I was taken down, just forced to move over and make room for the younger women.

In the time which we are living, there is an urgent need for "Praying Women." There are so many un churched people whose lives are yet to be touched; so many looking, searching, hoping for a way out. Our mission is for every soul who is ordained of God for this ministry to compel unbelievers to come and drink freely from the well of salvation. I challenge you today to use the insight and knowledge that you have been given to reach out for the lost souls.

Often I have cried, "Lord, you alone are my God, and I'm your servant. Use me, I pray, as an instrument of your love. Glorify yourself through me." God heard those prayers. He responded to the call of my heart and said, "Come unto me, all ye that labor and heavy laden and I will give you rest." Yes, I am resting in His bosom, bruised, and hurting, but fully delivered because with His stripes, I was and am healed. I'm a true Apostolic Mother; I don't regret the path I've taken on this journey. I now know that I could not have led the women of the Church of Our Lord off course because they are built on a solid foundation and can't be moved. Hallelujah!

BLEST. BROKEN. GIVEN.

CHAPTER NINETEEN

SUMMARIES OF THREE OF ELMER L. TOWNS BOOKS

Praying the Lord's Prayer for Spiritual Breakthrough
Fasting for Spiritual Breakthrough
Biblical Meditation for Spiritual Breakthrough

"And ye shall know the truth, and the truth shall make you free. John 8:32

Towns, Elmer L. *Praying the Lord's Prayer for Spiritual Breakthrough:* Ventura: Regal Books, 1997

Author Information

Dr. Elmer L. Towns is a college and seminary professor, an author of popular and scholarly works (the editor of two encyclopedias), a popular seminar lecturer, and dedicated worker in Sunday school, and has developed over twenty resource packets for leadership education.

He began teaching at Midwest Bible College, St. Louis, Missouri, for three years and was not satisfied with the textbooks so he began writing his own. He has published over one hundred books which are listed in the Library of Congress. Seven books are listed in the Christian Booksellers Best Selling List and several have become accepted as college textbooks.

He is also the 1995 recipient of the coveted Gold Medallion Award which was awarded by the Christian Booksellers Association for writing the Book of the Year. He is Vice President of Liberty University in Lynchburg, Virginia, and is Dean of the University's School of Religion.

149

His personal education includes a B.S. from Northwestern College, a M.A. from Southern Methodist University, and a Th.M. from Dallas Theological Seminary, an MRE from Garrett Theological Seminary, and a D.Min. from Fuller Theological Seminary. He is married to Ruth; they have three children and ten grandchildren.

Content Summary

Always say the Lord's Prayer with reverential attention, remembering that we have received it from our Divine Redeemer Himself. The Lord's Prayer includes everything you need to ask when you talk to God. This prayer can change your life. This book is devotional literature, inspirational, nonfiction, spiritual disciplines, and spiritual formation. Dr. Towns is teaching us how to pray as Jesus taught His disciples to pray and he does so by examining each line of the Lord's Prayer.

Dr. Towns desired a more powerful prayer life and shared his desire with Dr. Yonggi Cho. Dr. Towns his book, *Praying the Lord's Prayer for Spiritual Breakthrough*, at his home in the Blue Ridge Mountains, Virginia, in the spring of 1997. He stated his purpose for writing this book was so that when one daily experiences the Lord's Prayer, that person can *"touch God";* but more importantly so that right here and now…*"God can touch you"*. "I wrote this book to help you talk to God…using the Lord's Prayer" (Page 20).

The author states the Lord's Prayer contains a short Preface and Seven Petitions. The words: *Our Father who art in Heaven* are called the Preface. The author reminds us that God is our Father, and that He is so good and so worthy of veneration and there is no earthly father like Him. He states that we, therefore, ought to pray to Him with a childlike reverence, love and confidence.

This book contains eleven chapters and the Appendices A, B and C. The Seven Petitions are explained in chapters three through ten. When a person prays the Lord's Prayer, they have covered every type of petition that will touch every aspect of their lives. After each chapter, there is a Prayer Check List and space for journaling. Each chapter in this book includes suggestions about what experiences and impressions regarding one's prayer life that they should write about.

The author does an awesome job of presenting the best applications of the Lord's Prayer with practical insights. This prayer is the best known prayer in Christianity. The Lord's Prayer is not a prayer just to be repeated, but a pattern to enable us to include everything we are required to pray when we talk to God (Page 216). The book reminds us that prayer is communication with God. Because God is personal, all people can offer prayers. The Lord's Prayer and sometimes called the Disciples' Prayer was given to the Disciples who were believers. However, sinners who have not trusted Jesus Christ for their salvation remain alienated from God. So while unbelievers may pray, they do not have the basis for a rewarding fellowship with God. They have not met the conditions laid down in the Bible for effectiveness in prayer.

Dr. Towns states that if a person prays the Lord's Prayer daily, they will receive seven things that will change their lives and redirect their future. He goes on to write that the Lord's Prayer is the greatest prayer taught to us by the greatest Person for the greatest breadth of requests.

Dr. Towns reveals the power of prayer in his fascinating look at the Lord's Prayer. Each chapter examines a line from the Prayer, revealing power points for every believer who desires a more dynamic prayer life. He said, "What would you say if you were ushered into the throne room of God with only one minute to request everything you need, but didn't know how to put it into words? The Lord's Prayer includes everything you need to ask when you talk to God...it is a model prayer that teaches us how to pray."

Evaluation

The journey through *Praying the Lord's Prayer for Spiritual Breakthrough* is an excellent source of comfort, courage and strength. Daily praying the Lord's Prayer is a pathway to His presence. Carefully studying and reading this book will transform your life. You will walk closer to God, and you will receive many answers to prayer.

The author said that he did not write this book to examine the meaning of each phrase of the Lord's Prayer. He stated that one could gain some deep insights into the Lord's Prayer from this book. He wrote this book to help one talk to God by using the Lord's Prayer. This evaluation shows how he achieved his intended purpose by what he wrote.

What was unique, significant and interesting about this book is the way the author captured the reader's attention by using easy to read, understandable words and a simple style of writing. This book gave a pattern of a model prayer for daily living that, if followed correctly, will give tremendous rewards.

Anyone who wants a closer walk with the Lord should read this book. The excellent way the prayer is broken down and dissected is enlightening. It is not to be read like a novel, but as a study or reference book. Dr. Towns' focus on practical means of spiritual formation allows him to teach precept by precept, and line upon line. The book contains Biblical, Scriptural and theological information. Furthermore, it really increases ones desire to pray more often. Reading this book, can give an overwhelming experience with the Lord. The reader can now understand the power that is behind praying the Lord's Prayer.

This very insightful literary work gives a true understanding of asking God to guide your steps throughout the day as you communicate with Him through the Lord's Prayer. It can both challenge and change your life by giving principle methods of drawing an active and effective prayer life.

The implementation of these concepts into his ministry he/she will be blessed and those whom he touches will also reap the benefit. A quick survey of the Scriptures indicates numerous commands for Christians to pray. "Call unto me, and I will answer thee, and show thee great and mighty things, which thou knowest not" (Jer.33:3). "Pray without ceasing" (I Thess. 5:17). "Be careful for nothing; but in everything by prayer and supplication with thanksgiving let your requests be made known unto God" (Phil 4:6). Prayer clearly has a basic place in God's program. It enables believers to unite with God's purposes. Through prayer, people are dealing directly with God. Prayer is the channel through which they labor to win others to Christ.

Praying the Lord's Prayer for Spiritual Breakthrough accomplishes its goal because it was a *"spiritual break through"* for this reader. Jesus is our example and authority in prayer because He lived a life of prayer. Prayer was so important to Him that He taught His disciples to pray; which is the reason for this book. Jesus took time to show His disciples how to compose their prayer. This book shows that as we look into God's Word, the importance of prayer is quite clear. We find that prayer was both commanded and exemplified in the Bible.

What is good about this book? It tells us how Jesus wants us to pray; it is an explanation of the Lord's Prayer. It greatly contributes to a person's understanding of the subject of prayer. The Lord's Prayer sums up the teaching of Jesus. It is also a prayer that offers the grace of Jesus, His reverence for God, His childlike confidence in His Father and His power to go bravely through life no matter adversity He faced. When we pray His prayer, His Spirit becomes our own!

Through this reading, things that weren't visible were learned and have been repeated many times. They now awaken and stimulate. There is now praise, petition and a yearning to draw nearer to God through just talking to Him. Remember the words of the old proverb: *"Prayer is the key, but faith opens the door"*. Now we know how to use the key and are encouraged to share this knowledge with others.

The author's conclusion is that The Lord's Prayer is. . . .

✓ Talking,
✓ listening,
✓ opening up,
✓ loving,
✓ meditating,
✓ asking,
✓ magnifying,
✓ thinking,
✓ changing,
✓ waiting,
✓ confessing,
✓ worshiping,
✓ exalting,
✓ enjoying. . .

GOD.

By Elmer L. Towns

1. The Fasts God Chooses (Isaiah 58:6-8). Fasting is less important than doing God's will.

    This chapter covered the nine fasts God can use.

2. The Disciples Fast (Matthew 17:21). A private fast, achieving freedom from addictions or from besetting sins.

3. The Ezra Fast (Ezra 8:23). A corporate fast to "undo the heavy burdens." Inviting God into the problem, asking His solution, inviting everyone involved to be a part of the solution.

4. The Samuel Fast (I Samuel 7:6). Samuel fasted for Revivals and Soul winning exemplifies fasting as a symbol not our own power to move God by abstaining from food, but of our faith in His power to bring Revival.

5. The Elijah Fast (I Kings 19:48). Is an ongoing fast for a length of time for breaking emotional habits and negative mental problems.

6. The Widows Fast (I Kings 17:16). Is a not long fast, just missing one or two meals. When we focus on the needs of others as we sacrifice our own physical needs the Lord will bless.

7. The Saint Paul Fast (Acts 9:9). Is a three day fast with nothing to eat or drink for wisdom and decision making.

8. The Daniel Fast (Daniel 1:8). This fast consist of no meat, no sweets and no bread for a set

155

period of time, about three weeks. It is for physical health and healing. This fast is what my Church use a lot.

9. The John the Baptist Fast (Luke 1:15). No strong drinks. This fast is for those who want to be good influences, or for those who have not had good testimonies, but want to be influential for God.

10. The Esther Fast (Esther 4:16; 52). It is a corporate three day and night fast with nothing to neither eat nor drink. Fasting for protection from the evil one.

This book gives the biblical reasons for fasting (going without food or drink voluntarily for a period of time) and introduces nine biblical individual fasts which are designed for a specific physical and spiritual outcome. The author states from the very beginning, that before the Fall of Man, our bodies were probably designed to take periodic rests from food. The seventh day was designed for rest; the digestive system needs rest just as much as the rest of the body. (Page 176).

The Impact and Implementation of this Book in my Life

I can now put into practice the different types of fasts that I have read about. For protection I will do what Ezra did or like Daniel the prophet who fasted for the fulfillment of God's promises. Being a widow myself, I was impacted with the knowledge of the Widow's Fast.

Before reading this book, fasting was already a weekly part of my spiritual lifestyle. However, this book increased my knowledge of the different types, methods, reasons and purposes for fasting. I believe fasting is the most powerful spiritual discipline of the Christian disciplines. I also believe that fasting is one of the most neglected spiritual admonitions. I know through fasting and prayer, the Holy Spirit can transform my life. It is exciting to realize that awesome powers can be released through me as I fast through the enabling of the Holy Spirit, as I fast for a spiritual breakthrough.

From the knowledge that I have gained through the reading of this book and according to Scripture, personal experience and observation, I am convinced that when God's people fast with the proper Biblical motive – seeking God's face – with a broken, repentant, and contrite spirit, God will hear from Heaven and heal our lives, our churches, our communities, our nation and world. Fasting and prayer can bring about revival – a change in the direction of our nation, the nations of earth and the fulfillment of the Great Commission.

I will use this book as my personal guide to biblical fasting. Now I know how to start, what to expect physically and spiritually, and how to terminate a fast. This book covered any questions or concerns I may have had about fasting.

SUMMARY OF THE BOOK:

BIBLICAL MEDITATION FOR SPIRITUAL BREAKTHROUGH
– By Elmer L. Towns

Dr. Towns states that, "Because of what I have experienced in my own life through the discipline of meditation, I wanted to write this book to help others experience their own spiritual breakthrough." Meditation is a close and continued thought; pondering; reflection. He goes on to say that, "Christian meditation is about God. It is meditation that will change your life because you focus on God, and when you experience God, and it is God who changes you."

This book focuses on the positive biblical ideas of meditation and the ten biblical ways to meditate and draw closer to the Lord. Dr. Towns uses ten key models for biblical practice of this discipline. David, Mary the mother of Jesus, St. John the beloved disciple, Joshua, St. Paul, Timothy, Haggai, Asaph, Malachi and Korah were the ten individuals that were highlighted in this book. The book examined these ten different persons and how each meditated on God.

He outlines the biblical principles that grew out of each of these ten models and suggests practical steps to help one incorporate meditation into their life.

In this book Dr. Towns, shows that Christian meditation is not about methods, positions, mantras, formulas or false religions. It is the rediscovering the lost art of meditating on the things of God, His character, His Word, His creation and His amazing redeeming work in one's own life. He shows that meditation is a dynamic process that will change your thought life, encourage your growth in character and service.

Through his writing, Dr. Towns urges us to slow down and catch up with our loving Father through meditation and allow Him to change our lives to His glory. He also gives many Scriptures on which to meditate and some to memorize.

The impact and implementation of this book in my life was a spiritual breakthrough. I am alone a great deal, but I have trained myself to think pleasant thoughts. The Scripture, Philippians 4:8, is one that I use "…think on these things." I usually say "I am daydreaming" because I am wrapped up, tangled up and tied up in my thoughts, to the point that I'll just start "murmuring," "sighing," or "moaning." I can completely close out my surroundings and be in the presence of the Lord through my thoughts. I am experiencing the 12th chapter of

Ecclesiastes; my hearing and sight are not as keen as they once were, but within my thoughts I don't have this problem. I never called this action "meditation" until after reading this book. Now I can claim I know how to meditate according to biblical practice, just like the ten models which were featured in this book.

By studying this book I have learned how to correctly meditate on Jesus Christ and I am now on a higher level in my spiritual walk and communication with Christ. I feel that I have a deeper and more meaningful relationship with Christ.

BLEST. BROKEN. GIVEN.

CHAPTER TWENTY

WOMEN WORKING TOGETHER TO MAKE A DIFFERENCE A HIGH CALL FOR SUCH A TIME AS THIS NOW IS THE TIME

"Now the God of patience and consolation grant you to be like minded one toward another according to Christ Jesus: That ye may with one mind and one mouth glorify God, even the Father of our Lord Jesus Christ." Romans 15:5, 6

My first remembrance of the Ministers' and Deacon Wives' Guild of the Church of Our Lord Jesus (COOLJC) was in October 1970 in Sequin, Texas at an International Women's Council. The late Mother Ethel Mae Bonner was the President of the Guild and she had planned a luncheon at the hotel where most of the delegates were staying. Near the end of the IWC session she asked if someone would drive her back to the hotel. I agreed to chauffeur this Woman of God with a joyful spirit. I felt it was an honor and I was so excited. My excitement soon changed to embarrassment because no one attended the luncheon. I sat there with Mother Bonner and watched the ice cubes in the glasses turn into water. Many years later that image is still with me. The tables were set, the servers ready, and Mother Bonner gracefully waited; but no one came. Was this an example Women of God working together to make a difference?

I have another recollection of the Guild was when Mother Ethel Steadman being appointed President. The late Mother Grace Spellman was the secretary. That August, at the Holy Convocation, Mother Steadman presided at her first business meeting. After much discussion about our colors, my suggestion of green and gold won. I explained that green was for growth, peace and tranquility. The gold stood for dynasty because we are daughters of the King. The late Mother Mae Solomon suggested that we have a badge made of these colors. She stated that after a while our suitcases will be full of nothing but uniforms. We agreed on the badge. Dr. Celeste Ash Johnson, Sister Jerlease Smith and I were asked to design the pin. Mother Peters, Mother Steadman and I came up with the different criteria for awards and named them after the past Women Auxiliary President. Was this an example of Women of God working together to make a difference?

The next Convocation, Mother Steadman shocked us all by showing up in a gold a-line dress with a green scarf and hat. Mother Bonner was in Africa at the time when the Guild decided on the green and gold colors. She stated that while picking up "pine cones" that were brown and green, the name Golden Pine Reception was given to her. It seems like the Lord was working in the United States and Africa at the same time. Was this an example of Women of God working together to make a difference?

My thoughts and remembrance will not allow me to think of the history of the Ministers' and Deacons' Wives Guild without recalling the great contributions that Dr. Celeste Johnson gave during its inception. She worked diligently with each President. When it was her season to be elevated, the voting process changed. Instead of voting on the slate of officers as was done in time past, nominations were now going to be accepted from the floor. Was this an example of Women of God working together to make a difference?

I cannot forget the sweat and the tears, the agony and the fears, the pain and sometimes sorrow; but I can remember to the joy and the laugher, the songs, praises, strides and the gains. For through all of this, Christ has brought us to a higher calling for such a time as this.

We must remember the pioneers of the Guild whose shoulders we are standing on and whose seats we are sitting in. We must not rest on our laurels. We must put our shoulders to the wheel and work together in order to make a difference. The Lord is calling us to plant our feet on higher ground.

We must remain appreciative of our pioneers, as well as, the rich legacy and foundation from which we came. This is an Apostolic foundation that was not built on the land of the earth; neither was it built on any man made material of this world. Rather it was built on the blood and promise of Jesus Christ. Therefore, we are standing firm on a solid foundation. It is a foundation that has been tried by fire. This foundation was crucified on the cross and buried. Yet, it is a foundation that arose with all power in His hand and is the Chief Cornerstone of our existence.

I therefore challenge you to uphold the standards of Holiness. Women of God, we must work together to make a difference as we galvanize the whole Word, while reaching for souls. Walk, think, dress and act like you are daughters of the King. Don't give up or compromise now; we've come too far. Now is high time to learn how to work together for such a time as this. We are not victims when things go wrong in our lives. It is all in the plan of the Lord and not the Devil, whom we give so much credit to, when we should be glorifying the Lord.

In order to make a difference, we must do all we can to keep harmony and oneness of the Spirit. It is our duty to keep or observe that unity, recognize it as real and act upon it in the binding power of peace. We may be

163

many members, but we are still just one body and that one body has only one Spirit. He that hath not the Spirit of God is none of His. The fourth chapter of Ephesians tells us about the unity of the Spirit; all believers are one in the Spirit. Always remember that we are women of unity. Together we stand, divided we will surely fall. We must work together for the perfecting of the Body of Christ.

We are approaching the coming of the Lord, and in order to make the Rapture, we must survive. It's so much easier when we work together. Learn how to encourage your sister, lift her up in prayer. Show her love, be patient and kind, be forgiving, and if she should happen to fall, extend your hand to her and lift her up. Let her know that she can make it, for no temptation has overtaken us that is not common to us. The Lord will provide a way to escape.

Martha did not like Mary sitting at the feet of Jesus, instead of helping her. But she did not "attack" her sister, but she told the Lord. Don't wrestle with your sister, tell the Lord about her and doing that will make a difference.

By studying the lives of the women in the Bible, the good and the not so good, we have a message for the contemporary women of today. We can learn from their experiences, their joys and sorrows, their weaknesses and their strengths and how they worked together to make a difference. Just think about those women of the Bible who gave their handmaids to their husbands in order to make a difference. What about Ruth and Naomi? Queen Vashti and Esther? Yes, there must be Vashti women to make room for the Esther women; just make sure you're coming and not going. We are Women of God working together to make a difference.

Therefore, my beloved sisters, we must be steadfast, unmovable, always abounding in the work of the Lord;

for as much as we know so that our labor will not be in vain. We must live our faith with all our heart, mind, soul and strength, regardless of the cost.

Now is the time for us to wake up and be about our Father's business. Let us awake to sacrifice and self-denial. To give, to sacrifice, is to be like Christ. To change the world is to be totally divine and that is what it will take for the women of God working together in order to make a difference.

To effectively make a difference, an individual must first give herself to Christ and then to the church; thus enabling the minister to assist her in finding her rightful place in the Kingdom of God. Consequently, the individual will then become aware of God's Divine Purpose in the salvation of her soul. Moreover, the specific function desired by God for that individual can then be fully realized. The Apostolic Doctrine must be conformed to as it relates to the role of the helpmate.

What have you given or what have you done or said to change the face of the world and touch others with your life? Each of us should try to leave the world a better place than it was when we came into it. It was Bishop R. C. Lawson, the Establishmentarian of COOLJC, who expressed a desire that we should "Add to It" and improve upon what he left. The Lord is calling upon each individual and commands us to leave conditions better than we found them.

In conclusion, I challenge Guild members to remember your theme song:

One Day at a Time

"One Day at a Time, Lord Jesus; that's all I'm asking of you; Lord, give me the strength; to do every day what I have to do;

Yesterday's gone, Lord Jesus; and tomorrow may never be mine; That's why I say "show me the way; One Day at a Time.

I'm only human but I'm just a woman; Help me see all I can be and all that I am; Show me the stairway that I have to climb;

And for my sake, help me to take One Day at a Time. Lord you remember when you walked among men; Looking below, Lord Jesus, you now it's worse now than then.

They're pushing and shoving and crowding my mind; But by thy grace, we'll win the race One Day at a Time."

CHAPTER TWENTY-ONE

GOD COUNTS

"To everything there is a season, and a time to every purpose under the Heaven" (Ecclesiastes 3:1).

AGE RALLY (1 to 100)
A DOLLAR ($1.00) FOR EACH YEAR SINCE YOUR BIRTH

Certain numbers have certain significance and meaning throughout the Bible. Find your AGE within the Scriptures and prepare a 2 minutes explanation of your age using a Scripture. For example, if your age is 72 (70 plus 2): It is recorded in Luke 10:1, 17 "After these things the Lord appointed other *seventy* also, and sent them *two* and *two* before His face into every city and place, whither He Himself would come." " And the *seventy* returned again with joy, saying, Lord even the devils are subject unto us through thy name."

You could use: The 70 Nations in Genesis 10; the 70 Souls in Genesis 46:26; the 70 Elders in Exodus 24:1; the 70 Weeks of Daniel 9:24. For the number *two* Matt. 18:16; John 8:17; Mark 6:7; Acts 1:10; Hebrews 6:17-18 and 1 Timothy 3:15 Here the Church is identified as *two*, the Pillar and ground of truth a faithful servant and witness.

If you are in your 80's, you can use the Scriptures showing 40 years wandering in the wilderness plus the 40 days it rain during the flood plus the additional numbers.

NUMBERS AND MEANING:

1. **UNITY; NEW BEGINNINGS:** Matt. 19:5 *"And they twain shall be one flesh";* Zech. 14:9 *"there shall be one Lord...name one";* John 17:11 *"that they may be one";* I Tim. 2:5 *"for there is one God...one mediator..."*

2. **DIVISION; UNION; WITNESSING:** Gen. 1:4 *"and God divided* the Light from the darkness"; WITNESS Matt. 18:16 "that in the mouth of two or three witnesses."

3. **PERSONALITY; Father, Son, Holy Ghost – GODHEAD IN MANIFESTATION.**
   - Beast
   - False
   - Prophet
   - Devil
   - Trinity

RESURRECTION– Jonah-Christ...3rdday. DIVINE COMPLETENESS AND PERFECTION

4. **CREATION; THE WORLD; CREATIVE WORKS:** Seasons, direction, winds, four-footed Beast treads the earth. Four-beast Governments to rule world. Four elements, four divisions of day season of the moon.

5. **GRACE; GOD'S GOODNESS; PENTATEUCH (1ˢᵗfive books);** Tabernacle build on N. 5; first five books-foundation; five O.T.; offerings: burnt, peace, sin, trespass, meat.

6. **MAN'S NUMBER; WEAKNESS of MAN; MANIFESTATION of SIN, EVILS of SATAN**: Man created on 6th day, Man's labor is 6 days one day short of God's Perfection; number of Anti-Christ 666 (see Rev. 13:18).

7. **SPIRITUAL COMPLETE; FATHER PERFECTION; RESURRECTION:** 7 days cycle complete; seven Dispensations; in book of Revelation (#7-59 times) 7 appears at least 700 times in the Bible, (It is 4-earth's number plus 3-Trinity).

8. **NEW BEGINNINGS; RESURRECTION, NEW ORDER:** Gen. 17:12 circumcised 8 day. Day Christ arose NEW BIRTH in Rom. Chapter 8: Holy Spirit mentioned 19 times.

9. **FRUIT of the SPIRIT; DIVINE COMPLETENESS from the FATHER:** Gal. 5:22-23 nine Fruit mentioned. After God is given His tenth, Man has 9 parts left. Abraham was 99 years old, Sarah 90 when Isaac was born.

10. **LAW & RESPONSIBILITY; TESTIMONY: 10** Commandments; 10 Virgins. It also is a complete number 10 Lepers were cleansed. 10 Kingdoms will

confederate in the tribulation period. After 10 plagues the Egyptian drowned.

11. **INCOMPLETENESS; DISORDER and JUDGMENT:** 11 disciples after Judas left. 11 stars bowed down-Gen. 37:9.

12. **GOVERNMENTAL COMPLETION and PERFECTION:** 12 tribes of Israel; 12 gates to the New Jerusalem; 12 months in a year.

13. **REST**

14. **LOVE**

15. **VICTORY**

16. **BONDAGE**

17. **FAITH**

18. **REDEMPTION**

19. **EXCEEDING SINFULNESS of SIN**

20. **LIGHT**

21. **DEATH**

22. **THE PRIESTHOOD**

23. **REPENTANCE; THE FORGIVENESS of SINS**

24. **THE GOSPEL of CHRIST**

25. **PREACHING of the GOSPEL**

26. **ETERNAL LIFE**

27. **DEPARTURE**

28. **BLOOD of CHRIST; DEDICATION**

29. **OFFSPRING**

30. **COVENANT**

31.	PROMISE
32.	NAMING of a SON
33.	HOPE
34.	ENEMY
35.	THE WORD of OUR FATHER
36.	SLAVERY
37.	DISEASE
38.	TRIALS; PROBATION; TESTING'S
42.	ISRAEL'S OPPRESSION; FIRST ADVENT
44.	JUDGMENT of the WORLD
45.	PRESERVATION
50.	HOLY SPIRIT; PENTECOST
60.	PRIDE
70.	PUNISHMENT and RESTORATION of ISRAEL;
100.	ELECTION; CHILDREN of the PROMISE
119.	SPIRITUAL PERFECTION and VICTORY 7*17=119
120.	DIVINE PERIOD of PROBATION
144.	THE SPIRIT GUIDED LIFE
200.	INSUFFICIENCY
600	WARFARE
666.	ANTICHRIST

777.   CHRIST

888.   HOLY SPIRIT; THE SUM of TREE of LIFE

1000 DIVINE COMPLETENESS and FATHER'S GLORY

4000 SALVATION of the WORLD THROUGH the BLOOD of THE LAMB (Those who choose between Christ and Antichrist) DECEPTION of ANTICHRIST; SECOND ADVENT

Some examples from the Companion Bible:

FOUR – Denotes *creative works,* and always has reference to the material creation, as pertaining to the *earth,* and things "under the sun," and things terrestrial.

SEVEN – Denotes *spiritual perfection.* It is the hallmark of the Holy Spirit's work. He is the Author of God's Word, and seven is stamped on it as the watermark is seen in the manufacture of paper. He is the Author and Giver of *life;* and seven is the number which regulates every period of Incubation and Gestation, in insects, birds, animals, and man.

EIGHT – Denotes resurrection, regeneration; a new beginning or commencement. The eighth is a new first; hence the octave in music, color, days of the week. It is the number which has to do with the Lord, who rose on the eighth or new "firstday." This is, therefore, the *dominical* number. By Gem atria (the addition of the numerical value of the letters together) the Greek letters for Jesus makes the numbers 888. It or its multiple is impressed on all that has to do with the Lord's Names, the Lord's People, and the Lord's Works.

The Number Seventy

The number seventy is another combination of two perfect numbers, *seven* and *ten.* We have seen something of the significance of their *sum* under the number *Seventeen;* their product is no less significant.

As compared with the *sum* of two numbers, the product exhibits the significance of each in an intensified form. Hence 7 x 10 signifies *perfect* spiritual order carried out with all spiritual power and significance. Both *spirit* and *order* are greatly emphasized.

The Seventy Nations

The seventy nations which peopled the earth are set forth with a particularity which shows the importance of the fact (see Genesis 10).

The Seventy Souls of Genesis 46

The seventy souls of Genesis 46 are marked not only by the perfection of spiritual truth, as seen by the multiple of 7, but by the perfection of Divine order, as seen in the multiple of 10, seventy being 7 x 10.

We stop not to notice the number given in Acts &:14, which is different because it refers to a different classification, viz., **all his kindred,"** which amounted to 75. In Genesis 46:26, God is speaking to another class, viz. only those **"which came out of his loins,"** these were seventy in number.

BLEST. BROKEN. GIVEN.

CHAPTER TWENTY-TWO

THE APOSTOLIC *"WOMEN OF PRAISE"* GOING THROUGH COMING OUT MOVING ON IN THE RIGHT DIRECTION

"There hath no temptation taken you but such as is common to man: but God is faithful who will not suffer you to be tempted above that ye are able; but will with the temptation also make a way to escape, that ye may be able to bear it."
I Corinthians 10:13

After *"Going Through"* life's trials and tribulation, *"Coming Out"* a stronger woman in Christ and *"Moving On"* in the right direction, we can claim our rightful place in the Lord. I am certain that as Women of God we have entered each of these passages at one time or another and have remained intact by trusting and believing in the WORD! My prayer is that this reading will make you aware of some of the trials that you have gone through, to give instructions on how to work them out, and place in your hearts the inspiration to go on with your life.

After Peter received the Holy Ghost, he became a ROCK fulfilling the prophecy of Christ and gave certain guidelines for the believers to follow. The central theme in his first epistle (letter) is victory over suffering. He declared that there is victory in the state of suffering, and that through the spiritual mind the flesh, is subdued.

In this epistle, Peter doesn't only give instruction; he leaves behind a legacy of hope for those ambitious individuals who desire to become great in the Lord. The first verse of the 4th chapter of 1st Peter states, *"For as much then as Christ hath suffered for us in the flesh arm yourselves likewise with the same mind: for he that hath*

175

suffered in the flesh hath ceased from sin." 12th verse, *"Beloved, think it not strange concerning the fiery trials which is to try you, as though some strange thing happen unto you." The 13th* verse states, *"But rejoice, in as much as ye are part takers of Christ's suffering, that, when his glory shall be revealed, ye may be glad also with exceeding joy."*

In order to grow in grace and in the knowledge of our Lord and Savior Jesus Christ, we must die daily, just as a planted seed must die and be cultivated in order for it to grow. When building a structure, the foundation must first be dug "down" before it goes up. Think about this: when a grain of sand accidentally makes its way into the softness of an oyster, it causes an annoying aggravation. Then the oyster secrets a substance to salve the aggravation. Eventually, because of this annoying grain of sand, a beautiful, priceless pearl is created. The beauty of a diamond is brought forth by constant pressure applied to an ugly piece of coal; thus, the ugly becomes the beautiful. The wriggly caterpillar, its icky presence appalling to so many, will someday become a beautiful butterfly. In time, even the tiny tadpole grows into the mighty bull frog. Change wills it so, and the law of compensation deems it necessary.

God's grace speaks of the lifelong process of the Spirit filled believer who reconciles herself to sitting on the Potter's Wheel so that the Lord can mold and make her for His Glory and Honor. The growth process is never appealing, but the results are extremely fruitful. No one wants to be in the valley; everyone wants to be on the mountain top. Do you know the soil in the valley is very rich? Rivers run in the valley, sweet grapes and apples grow in the valley. It takes valleys to make mountains. If you want to be fruitful, try spending more time in the valley. The Lord is in the valley. "Yes, though I walk through the valley of the shadow of death, I will fear no evil: for thou art with me."

176

When we can go through something, come out, move on and come to know the Lord, no mountain is too high nor valley too low. No weapon formed against us will prosper. When we least expect it, God will answer, for the prayers of the righteous man availed much. Like Aaron and Hur, we should hold up the tiring hands of our pastors, teachers, evangelists, missionaries, sisters and all who fight the good fight of faith.

The sixty-six books of the Bible are our sword to fight with. We have to know how to use our weapon, to be able to go through, come out and move on in the right direction. The Bible was written to the Jews, Gentiles and the Church of God therefore, we have to know how to rightly divide the Word of God. Apostolic Women of Praise, in order to teach the Word, we have to study the Word, live the Word, digest the Word and take pride in it.

Women of God, we have learned how to stuff and swallow any and everything. However, we also must learn how to release what the Lord have given us. We must acquire the freedom of expression based on our understanding. No longer, should we just sit, close our eyes, bow our heads, and just pray for a situation. It's time to "cry loud and spare not," to pull the covers off of the Devil. It's time to take a stand for righteousness. To pray with our eyes and heart open and wail before the Lord.

The Apostolic Women of Praise uses her salt, shines her light because she is a city that is on a hill and a Kingdom builder. If salt just sits, stands still, and not used for a period of time, it will become useless, not good for anything but to be thrown out and trampled under feet. It may be in the right place (on a table) and it the right type of container (salt shaker) but not used for the purpose it was made. Just think on the scripture that tells us to "wait on the Lord". Do you know what a waiter or waitress does? They serve people! Yes, we are saved to serve.

Just do something! Be like Habakkuk who stationed himself as a watchman to look at the nations, as God had commanded him. He cried out against violence, lawlessness, and the injustice that he saw all around him. Habakkuk did something when he was told to write the vision, not speak it, but write, and make it plain. Another he was told to arise; take up your bed, walk, and take up your cross and follow me. Some of us are standing still, marking time and accomplishing nothing. That makes the weight of our cross is a heavy burden. The Lord has promised that His burdens are light. Our burdens may seem heavy because maybe we are just marking time. We should all know that a load seems lighter when you are moving rather than when you are standing still.

The following are Scriptures that inform the Apostolic Women of Praise how she can successful go through, come out and move on in the right *direction*. It is recorded in St John 10:27: *"My sheep hear my voice, and I know them and they follow me, and I will give them eternal life."* Jesus describes three characteristics of His sheep: (1) They hear His voice (2) He knows them, and (3) they follow Him. Ephesians 6:16-17 states *"Above all, taking the shield of faith, wherewith ye shall be able to quench all the fiery darts of the wicked, And take the helmet of salvation, and he sword of the Spirit, which is the Word of God."*

It is recorded in II Timothy 3:12: *"Yea, and all that live Godly in Christ Jesus shall suffer persecution."* Know this, that God's Grace is sufficient. Grace is God's unmerited favor toward us. The Scripture tells us to take unto us the whole armor of God that we may be able to "withstand" which means to stand against with determination successfully.

Jeremiah 9:17-18 states *"Thus saith the Lord of hosts, consider ye, and call for the mourning women, that they may come, and send for the cunning (skillful) women that they may come, and let them make haste, and take up a wailing for us, that our eyes may run down with tears, and our eyelids gush out with waters."* Here Jeremiah was told to call for the skillful, professional, wailing women. The women were called to sing laments when Josiah died. Here they are called to weep over the collapse of Jerusalem. There was urgency in summoning the skilled mourners to lead the people in tearful lament over the destruction of Judah. In this day and time the Lord is calling for the Apostolic Women of Praise to do likewise for the unbelievers. The three types of women that Jesus every called or sent for are the mourning women, the cunning women and the wailing women. The Apostolic Women of Praise must wail to the Lord and teach their daughters how to do the same.

Women of God, just how much time do you spend talking about what the Devil made you do? How much time do you spend in prayer complaining about what people are doing to you? Instead of giving God the glory for allowing you to stand, to go through, move on and getting to really know the Lord.

Good health is a blessing, but that not what makes you blessed. Prosperity is a blessing, but that not what makes you blessed. A good job and being able to pay all of your bills when they are due, is a blessing; but that is not what makes you blessed. Being blessed is having the favor of God over your life, His Grace to stand against wickedness, and to really know the Lord and understand His Glory and Victory.

Women of God, you must stay focused and keep your eyes on the prize. So what if you are being mistreated? So what you if were not invited to their home or can't ride in their new car? Get over it and move on. So what if you're not appreciated, respected or given any honor—get

179

over it and move on in the right direction. You've the Grace of God, His Favor, to overcome whatever is put before you. It takes a test to have a testimony.

Beloved, remember that because of God's strength, you can go through anything and not get stuck in the middle but come out and move on in the right direction in Jesus' Name. With God's help you're an overcomer. If you can try, just believe then you will receive all of the blessings that the Lord has in store for you. However, you must go through something, come through something and move on in the right direction.

CHAPTER TWENTY-THREE

HOW EVANGELISM AND DISCIPLESHIP WORK TOGETHER

"Go ye therefore, and teach all nations, baptizing them in the name of the Father, and of the Son and of the Holy Ghost: Teaching them to observe all things whatsoever I have commanded you: and, lo, I am with you always, even unto the end of the world. Amen." Matthew 28:19, 20

FOCUS ON WHO YOU'RE TRYING TO REACH, NOT WHO YOU'RE TRYING TO KEEP

Jesus' last command to *"make disciples"* (Matt. 28:19) should be the first concern of every church ministry and the individual Saint. The Lord loved the unsaved so much that He provided the means for their salvation (John 3:16), urged His disciples to pray for laborers for the harvest (Matt. 9:38), and empowered and appointed His disciples as witness (Acts 1:8). Although the message of the Gospel has not changed, there are different strategies in every generation which prove effective in reaching the lost for Christ. We need not hold onto traditional methods because "that's the way it has always been done." During this session the Women of God will be seeking how to examine new approaches and incorporate them into their evangelism strategy.

Evangelism refers to the practice of relaying information about a particular set of believers to those who do not hold those beliefs. The Scripture often describes "evangelism" as "spreading the Gospel."

THREE STAGES INVOLVED IN THE EVANGELISM PROCESS

First, begin with the *presence evangelism* in order to "win a hearing." Women of God we must have good testimonies and be interested in the needs of the lost. Our Godly lives will help motivate thc lost to give an honest hearing to the Gospel. The Gospel is good news of the death, burial and resurrection of our Lord and Savior Jesus Christ. Presence Evangelism stems from the biblical word or *"witness"* or *"testimony."* We can evangelize by living God-honoring lives before the lost. Hopefully, as non-believers witness the Women of God who are living distinct lifestyles, they will want to know more about the Gospel and ultimately come to Christ. This involves giving a testimony of what Christ has done in your life, or sharing your faith with others.

Next, we must *proclaim* the Gospel to the unsaved. Before people can be saved, they must hear the Gospel and understand its message. While witnessing the Women of God must not add works to the Gospel, nor must they dilute its obligations.

Finally, the Women of God must *persuade* people to receive Christ. At times Paul pleaded with tears (Rom. 9:2; 10:1), while at other times he persuaded as a trial lawyer often does (Acts 13:43).

Evangelism does not end when a person confesses the Holy Ghost. An effort must also be made to bond that convert to the church and to provide nurture and growth. This process is called *DISCIPLESHIP*, the guiding of individuals to grow into spiritual maturity and allow them to discover and use their gifts, talents and abilities in fulfillment of Christ's mission.

Just as a baby needs special attention as it grows toward physical maturity, so babes in Christ need others to help them grow toward spiritual maturity. A new Saint may become discouraged and fail to live for Christ if someone does not offer to help the new convert to grow spiritually.

Jesus wants our fruit to remain (John 15:16) *"Ye have not chosen me, but I have chosen you, and ordained you, that ye should go and bring forth fruit, and that your fruit should remain: that whatsoever ye shall ask of the Father in my name, he may give it you."* Disciplining new believers to maturity are essential if that goal is to be achieved. Disciplining men and women should be the priority around which our lives orientate. It shouldn't seem strange that our Lord would place such a high priority on discipline. After all, Jesus was simply asking His followers to do what He had done while He was with them. That is why they could understand it. His disciples had freely received and now they were to transmit what they had learned to others seekers of the Truth. Jesus Christ Himself said it in His final words before His ascension into Heaven to be on the right hand of God the Father (Matt. 28:19, 20). Matthew's account sums it up: *"Go ye therefore, and make disciples of all the nations, baptizing them into the name of the Father and of the Son and of the Holy Spirit: teaching them to observe all things, whatsoever I commanded you: and, lo I am with you always, even unto the end of the World."* "Go," "baptizing," and "teaching" are participles. This mean that these responsibilities derive their direction from the leading verb, *"make disciples."* Or as it might be translated, *"make learners of Christ."*

He spoke to believers and revealed to them that it was His plan for them to be. The voice of Evangelism in the beginning of the Dispensation of Grace, when He said: *"All power is given unto me in Heaven and in earth:* (Matt. 28:18); *""Ye shall receive power after that the Holy Ghost is come upon you: and ye shall be witness unto me both in*

Jerusalem, and in all Judaea, and in Samaria, and unto the uttermost part of the earth" (Acts 1:8).

As individuals learn of Him and follow the pattern of His life, they will invariably become disciples, and as their disciples, in turn, do the same, someday through multiplication the world will come to know Him whom to know aright is life everlasting.

Encouraging spiritual growth is the goal of discipleship. This process begins when a person trusts Christ as Savior and continues for an indefinite period of time. Discipleship is a lifelong process; we should always be growing in our relationship with Christ. In the weeks and months following a person's decision to trust Christ as Savior, the process of discipleship is of uttermost importance. During this time, the principles of growth need to become a part of the new believer's lifestyle. If new believers can be equipped and encouraged to develop habits of Bible study, prayer, fellowship, worship, ministry, and stewardship, they will experience rapid spiritual growth initially and continue to grow for years to come.

Evangelism and discipleship are not simply options for believers. It is a mandate for each and every believer and an essential element for living the Christian life. The Scriptures gives several reasons and motivations for saints, including the fact that Christ commanded it, that sinners need the Gospel, and that our love for Christ and for others should compel us toward that task.

Evangelism and discipleship should be the primary emphasis of the Church. As the Church strives to bring believers to maturity, neglecting the process of evangelism and discipleship will surely hinder the process. Church programs, Missionary Topics Service, Fellowship, and Community Service should be secondary concerns. A church that is not evangelistic will quickly become ingrown

184

and immobile. Each member must be encouraged to make evangelism and discipleship an integral part of their daily life.

The three E's that have proven effective for Evangelism and Discipleship are:

- **EXALT THE SAVIOR**--Jesus is to be lifted up. *"But I, when I am lifted up from the earth, I will draw all men to myself"* (John 12:32 NIV). How do we reach people for Christ? Lift up Jesus. It is He who draws people to Himself.

- **EQUIP THE SAINTS** – *"And He Himself gave some to be apostles, some prophets, some evangelists, and some pastor and teachers, for the equipping of the saints for the work of ministry, for the edifying of the body of Christ"* (Eph. 4:11-12, NKJV).

- **EVANGELIZE THE SINNER** – *"All authority in heaven and on earth has been given to me. Therefore go and make disciples of all nations, baptizing them in the name of the Father and of the Son and of the Holy Spirit, and teaching them to obey everything I have commanded you. And surely I am with you always, to the very end of the age"* (Matt. 28:18-20, NIV).

There must also be a holistic understanding of Evangelism and Discipleship as they relate to every function of the Church. Properly defined, we should not hesitate to reestablish them both as the purpose and priority of our congregation. Most of all, we should not forget the *harvest* principles, *plowing* through prayer, *planting* the Gospel seed and then the *harvest* will naturally come. Properly understood, the *harvest* is a natural outcome that can only be halted when the principles are ignored. In other words, the only way to kill the *harvest* is to not *plow* and *plant.* This may appear to be old fashioned.

Nevertheless, the principles are biblically sound and must never be ignored.

FOUR COMMITMENT STATEMENTS THAT ARE DESIGNED TO REFLECT THE HARVEST PRINCIPLES

The four accountability points are as follows:

1. Commit to having a daily quiet time and, as part of this, keeping a list of unsaved people and pray for them daily (*plowing).*

2. Commit to sharing your faith with at least one person each week (outside of the church setting) with the aim, as the Holy Spirit leads, to draw the net (*planting and harvesting).*

3. Commit to doing at least one significant "servant hood evangelism" activity per month in your community (*planting and sometimes harvesting).*

4. Commit to multiplying yourself by mentoring at least one person in your sphere of influence per year, in order to adopt these life principles.

While the Church is called to plow and plant, the harvesting is always the business of God. Man does not create the harvest, but if the fields are, as Jesus states in John 4:35 (NASB), "white for harvest," through the invitation, the preacher uniquely becomes a partner in the harvest with Christ. The Church has a responsibility to disciple new believers to maturity. They need to be taught how to grow spiritually through Bible study, prayer, fellowship, worship, ministry, and stewardship. Believers with special gifts which enable them to minister as equippers and encouragers will be especially valuable in this aspect of evangelism and discipleship. As Women of God, we need to invest ourselves in training new believers according to a plan using discipleship materials which will help new believers mature.

REFERENCES

Bible (KJV)

Coleman, Robert E.: *The Master Plan of Discipleship,* Grand Rapids, MI Baker Publishing Group, 1998

Falwell, Jonathan: *Innovate Church,* Nashville, Tennessee, B&H Publishing Group, 2008

Towns, Elmer L.: *Your Ministry of Evangelism, A Guide for Church Volunteers,*

(ETA), Wheaton, Illinois, Evangelical Training Association, 2004

BLEST. BROKEN. GIVEN.

CHAPTER TWENTY-FOUR

THE ROLE OF WOMEN IN MINISTRY

"But I suffer not a woman to teach, nor to usurp authority over the man, but to be in silence."
I Timothy 2:12

INTRODUCTION

Few issues are as controversial in religious circles as the role of women in ministry. Western culture has undergone a dramatic shift in its view of women in ministry. This shift has caused a rift within the church. Using content analysis, this research will highlight the varied philosophical perspectives of the role of the women in ministry. This paper will profoundly determine what this writer believes to be a sound conclusion of the role of the women in ministry, and the intent of I Timothy 2:9-15, as it relates to the role of women in the ministry. The Scripture, 1 Timothy 2:9, states *"I suffer not a woman to teach, nor to usurp authority over the man, but to be in silence"* (AV). Translation and interpretation of I Timothy 2:9-15 is crucial. It can release women to serve wherever in the ministry that God may call them, or hinder them from certain roles of service within the church.

According to the New Testament, women cannot be leaders in the church, but they can help their husbands lead. Women should concentrate their efforts in the sphere of the home, and they should concentrate in the areas of ministry and service to others. Fulfillment is in knowing one's assigned role and then doing it to the glory of God.

Thesis Statement

This paper will examine what the Bible says about women in ministry in I Timothy 2:9-15. It is an issue of biblical interpretation of the women in ministry as stated in I Timothy 2:9-15 within the confines of the Pastoral Epistles (1st and 2nd Timothy and Titus). I Timothy 2:9-15 is so often the pivotal one in controversy over the role of the women in ministry. This writer therefore believes that an extensive amount of pertinent information of this subject is necessary.

BODY

Paul relied on Timothy to help him establish leadership and make up the deficits in the church in Ephesus. From Macedonia, Paul wrote to encourage his "son" in faith. The central purpose of I Timothy is found in 3:15: "I write so that you may know how you ought to conduct yourself in the house of God, the pillar and ground of the truth." The Church is God's primary vehicle for accomplishing His work on earth. The Lord has ordained that men and women who have trusted Him as Savior should be involved in working out His will in local assemblies.

Clearly, woman has a role in the ministry, but scholars disagree as to what this role is within the local church setting. The views concerning the role of women in ministry are often broken down into two distinct groups: Those who believe women should be permitted to hold positions of pastoral authority in the church, is referred to as the "egalitarian" or "progressive" view. Those who believe that only men are permitted to hold such position in the church, is known as the "historic" or "traditional" view (Women Pastors/Preachers?).

Much of the problem over this difficult text is because so little is known about the lives and outlook of the women to whom Paul is addressing. The Jewish women were familiar with the law and understood what was expected of them by God. However, the new Christian Gentile women had no intimate knowledge of God's law. It was necessary for Paul to write and reiterate in all of his epistles God's order of things.

Today, we are experiencing the same problem that is persistent in the Church. The Church continues to draw into it men and woman who are largely unfamiliar with what God's law says and struggle with its requirements. They don't understand the necessity of order and God's will for the family. The Word of God proclaims, "A woman should learn in quietness and full submission. I do not permit a woman to teach or to have authority over the man, she must be silent" (I Timothy 2:11-12). As a result of the way mankind was created sin entered the world (Three Women: Sarah, Rebecca, and Jezebell).

In I Timothy 2:9-15, Paul is exhorting the women at Ephesus to be concerned about clothing themselves with godly character, good works and their love for the Lord, instead of wearing inappropriate clothes that draw attention to them when at worship and to learn in silence. This refers to the woman's attitude while learning, as should be true of all believers, Paul was cautioning women to learn with an attitude of submission that their beauty would be found in her godly character and her love for the Lord as demonstrated in all types of good works and her pray life. Paul is referring to being delivered from the desire to dominate by recognizing one's appropriate place in God's creation order (Bonner, W. L.)

In God's order of creation, Adam was formed first, before Eve. In ancient society the firstborn receives special privileges a double portion. According to the Law of Moses the term "firstborn" was used literally and figuratively, expressing a relationship, an inheritance, preeminence and privilege that God gives honor to the firstborn. These privileges were not given on the basis of inherent superiority but instead of being born first. I Corinthians 11: 9 states that the man was not created for the woman but the woman for the man.

The law was not amended or annulled in grace, it is law forever. The law is binding for all times. The woman was cursed and required to bear pain and suffer in child bearing. She is also made subject to man and the man is given ruler ship over her. This is especially true in terms of the relationship between man and woman. Apostle Paul states in I Corinthians 11:3, *"But I would have you know that the head of every man is Christ; and the head of the woman is the man; and the head of Christ is God."* Submission can be painful for many women but it is part of the curse, *"For he shall rule over thee"* (The Pastoral Epistles)

When Jesus Christ made it known to us through the epistles that "the Head of Christ is God," He affirmed God's order, and no one can alter it. The woman cannot be the head of the man under any circumstances. It is not God's Order. The head of the man is Christ, and the Head of Christ is God. One cannot remove Christ and put man; nor can one remove man and put woman. The Angel of the Church at Thyatira absolutely disregarded God's order and placed a prophetess over the ministers to control and manipulate them (Revelations 2:20-23) and was punished with great tribulations (Nicholas, D. R.).

Jesus Christ did not pick women to be one of the original twelve disciples, nor does the Board of Apostles, and nor does the Board of Bishops choose a woman. When Jesus Christ ascended He left women here that were more knowledgeable than some of His male disciples. They watched all of His miracles and heard His teachings. Also, they learned just as His male disciples learned God's message. They were not ignorant or dumb women. These were enlightened women who knew and understood the mind of God. These were not women who came out of the back woods. These were women who sat at His table and at His feet. They were with Him in His going out and His coming in.

They understood everything that the disciples understood and yet, He didn't place one of them on the Board of Apostles or on the Board of Bishops. Why not? It is because a woman was never in the priesthood and she could not be included in the discipleship of the New Testament. God knows how to run His business. We are the ones who don't understand how He runs His business. That is one reason why this text is still debated today. There are false prophets and prophetesses. There are people who do not understand God's order and as a result things are in His permissive will but not the Divine Will of God. Women are now being ordained as Bishops and Apostles. In many churches, women are in every type of position of authority. This is repulsive to God Almighty.

The following are some organizations that do not allow women to hold positions of pastoral authority within the local church:

The position of the University Presbyterian Church by the UPC Session of Elders of the role of women in the church is that women may not be Elders, but that women may serve in any capacity with the local church that any non-elder male might serve. The session of UPC would add to this that they believe this same limitation would also forbid women from shepherding men.

In summary, the position of University Presbyterian Church is as follows:

- Women and men are equal in the church – both have been gifted by God for ministry and are co-heirs of the grace of life.

- The Bible prohibits women from serving as Elders.

- Women may serve in any capacity in the church and may use their spiritual gifts in every way that any non-elder man may serve, except that women may not shepherd men. In addition, University Presbyterian Church is part of the Presbyterian Church in America, which only allows men to be ordained as deacons. Out of submission, UPC does not ordain women as Deacons.

With all its issues, the University Presbyterian Church desires to be biblical above all else. Their commitment is to the Bible as the authoritative Word of God. The Bible alone is their only infallible standard for what they believe and how they live. In its study of the Word of God, the Session of UPC saw errors in both the "traditional" and the "progressive" view of women. In the traditional model, women have been oppressed and marginalized. Yet, the progressive model obliterates the God-given differences of women and men. While the traditional model fails to give women the freedom to use their spiritual gifts fully with the Church, the progressive model ignores the Bible's teaching on the different ways in which men and women may serve in the Church (The Role of Women in the Church).

The Association of Vineyard Churches – This group only allows men to fulfill the office of elders and pastor, but allows women to "preach, teach, evangelize, heal, prophesy, counsel, nurture, administrate, and build up the flock of God" (The Position of University Church).

In 1978 Pearl Williams-Jones surveyed five major Pentecostal bodies and categorized them with respect to their treatment of women in ministry and leadership. The first category, consisting of churches who insist upon the subordination of women in ministry roles, actually comprises the overwhelming majority of black Pentecostals (Sanders, C. J.)

The assumption of the text I Timothy 1:9-15 is that the men in the Church at Ephesus where Timothy was pastor were hindering the progress of the Gospel either by their prayerlessness or by using their prayers improperly to make points in conflict (dissension). So, likewise, it is safe to assume that when Paul turns to the women in v. 9, his message to them is influenced by particular problems that had arisen in that church. It would appear that some of the Ephesus women were dressing not modest and being contentious about doctrine in ways that threatened to overturn proper order and authority in the Church. Paul's instructions to the Ephesians are intended to prevent these abuses so that the Church can function properly as the household of God (Oden, T. C.).

In the Scripture, I Timothy 2:9-15, Paul is targeting the struggle with the role of women in the ministry because we struggle with sin. The women in Ephesus were doing exactly the same thing as Eve – struggling against the authority of Godly men. Their focus was on themselves not God and what God would have for them. Paul is writing, in conduct, in times of instruction, in times of teaching, the attitude of Godly women. The actions of a Godly woman must come from a heart that is broken before God, eagerly seeking God and the things of God, obedience to God, in faith, in love, in sanctity with self-restraint (Kent, H. A.).

Even where structural prohibitions have been in effect, women nevertheless found ways to exercise their gifts of ministry and leadership to benefit of the entire

195

church. For example, some women evangelists and revivalists founded churches as is recorded in church history. In addition, male church leaders often reported in their spiritual biographies that they became converted in response to the ministry of female preachers and female revivalists.

CONCLUSION

It was not gender but spiritual gifts that qualified individuals to be acknowledged and honored. The person and congregational accounts passed down in written records and oral tradition placed a high value on the contribution of women and men to the most important goal of the church – salvation and holiness.

Elders are to be men (I Timothy 3:1-3). In I Timothy 2:11, Paul forbids women to "teach or have authority" over men. In I Corinthians 14:35-36, women are not to take part in determining whether a teacher is teaching sound doctrine. Paul's command for women to "keep silent in church" surely cannot mean that they may never speak publicly. That Scripture would contradict the eleventh chapter of I Corinthians where women are told to pray and prophesy. It means they are to keep silent when the prophets are judged. The passage that is often used to disempowered women is actually an empowering them.

Why does God call certain ones? Is it because they are inherently more worthy? That has never been the case. It is the same question: why did the Father rule while the Son submitted? The answer is that both were great and wise persons who did not resent the submission and rule pattern but rejoice in it (Nicholas, D. R.). Knowledge is important. Don't believe that lie that folks say, "What you don't know won't hurt you." What you don't know can kill you and what you know can free you. It's important for us to add knowledge to our lives as we grow and mature in God.

God has given us many avenues to increase our knowledge of Him and His ways, and **as we seek to learn more of Him, we are blessed and are a blessing to others.**

BIBLIOGRAPHY

Assemblies of God position paper. *"The Role of Women in Ministry as Described in Holy Scripture."* Gospel Publishing House, Springfield, MO August 1990

Baugh, S. M. *A Foreign World: Ephesus in the First Century, Essay In Women in the Church: A Fresh Analysis of* I Timothy 2:9-15,

Andreas J. Kostenberger, Thomas R. Schreiner and H. Scott Baldwin, Eds. Grand Rapids: Baker Books, 1995, pp. 19-50.

Andreas J. Kostenberger, Thomas R. Schreiner, H. Scott , eds. Grand Rapids: Baker Books, 1995, p.204.

Bonner, William L. *Three Women: Sarah, Rebecca, Jezebel.* Copyright 1993. Bowman, Ann L. *Women in Ministry: An Exegetical Study of I Timothy 2:11-15.* Bibliotheca Sacra, April-June 1992, p. 198.

Brown, Harold O. J. *The New Testament against Itself:* I Timothy 2:9-15 and the 'Breakthrough' of Galatians 3:28, *Essay in Women in the Church: A Fresh Analysis of* I Timothy 2:9-15.

Doriani, Daniel. *A History of the Interpretation of I* Timothy 2. Appendix 1 in *Women in the Church: A Fresh Analysis of* I Timothy 2:9-15, Andreas J. Kostenberger, Thomas R. Schreiner and H. Scott Baldwin, eds. Grand Rapids Baker Books, 1995, pp. 213-267.

Guthrie, Donald, *The Pastoral Epistles.* Tyndale New
Testament Commentaries.

Grand Rapids: Wm. B. Eerdmans Publishing Co., 1990, p.
86.

Hogan/Albach, *They Tells Them So: "Evangelical Group
Embraces Gener"* Egalitarianism as the Only
Scriptural Way. *The Dallas Morning News,* June 16,
2001.

Kent, Homer A., Jr. *The Pastoral Epistles.* Winona Lake:
BMH Books, 1986, p. 106.

Kroeger, Richard & Catherine. *I Suffer Not a Woman.*
Grand Rapids, MI. Baker Books, 2993

Nicholas, David R. *What's a Woman to Do...In the Church?*
Scottsdale, AZ. Good Life Production, Inc., 1979, p.
107.

Oden, Thomas C. *First and Second Timothy and Titus.*
Louisville. John Knox Press, 1989, p. 116.

Robinson, Bruce A. *Women Clergy in Orthodox and
Protestant Christianity And other Religions.*

Sanders, Cheryl J. *"History of Women in the Pentecostal
Movement."* Cybejournal For Pentecostal-
Charismatic Research.

Schreiner, Thomas R. *An Interpretation of I Timothy 2:9-15:
A Dialogue with Scholarship.* Essay in *Women in the
Church: A Fresh Analysis of I Timothy 2:9-15,*
Andreas J. Kostenberger, Thomas R. Schreiner and
H. Scott Baldwin, Eds. Grand Rapids. Baker Books,
1995, p. 122.

Steig, Shelly. *Finding the Right Church: A Guide to
Denomination Beliefs.*

Iowa Falls, LA. World Bible Publishers, Inc., 1997, p. 110.

Stimson, Eva, editor. *"Together on Holy Ground.".* Geneva, Switzerland. WCC Publication, 1999, p. 21.

University Presbyterian Church (UPC) Standards. *"The Role of the Women in Church."*

"What The Bible Says About The Role of Women." http://www.rapidnet.com/ Jbeard/bdm/Psychology/eccl/women.htm

"Women Pastors/Preachers? What Does the Bible Say About

http://www.gotquestions.org/women-pasors.html

Yarbrough, Robert W. *The Hermeneutics of* I Timothy 2:9—15, *Essay in Women In the Church: A Fresh Analysis of I* Timothy 2:9-15, Andreas J.
Kostengerger,

R. Schreiner and H. Scott Baldwin, Eds. Grand Rapids. Baker Books, 1995, pp.167-171.

Zikmund, Barbara Brown, Adair T. Lummis, and Patricia M.

CHALLENGES TO THE FLORIDA REGIONAL MOTHER OF THE YEAR

"The Saved Mother and her Relationship to her Son"

The assignment given to me tonight is to speak for 15 minutes on the topic of *The Saved Mother and her Relationship to her Son*. The definition that I would like to use for a saved mother is a spirit- filled mother that does justly, loves mercy, and walks humbly with her God. This definition describes me. Therefore, I could give stories about my relationship with my sons. The Lord has blessed me with two biological sons, five grandsons, and five Godsons. Each one has different characteristics. They all profess Christ as their personal savior and are doing great Kingdom Work for their Master in different parts of the vineyard.

My firstborn was consecrated to the Bishopric before the age of 50. In honor of his father to continue the legacy of the late Bishop Ruel Bartholomew McCoy, who was a strong supporter of this Mother of the Year Fellowship; he stopped using his given first name "Marcus" and started using his middle name, which was his father's first name "Ruel." He did this so there will be only one Bishop Ruel McCoy. He is an honorable servant. Moreover, I do not believe one can find a "bigger" or "better" Deacon in COOLJC than my second son, Deacon Luke Bartholomew McCoy. I could talk extensively about our relationship and the many outstanding accomplishments of my sons, grandsons, and Godsons. However, because the Bible is our roadmap to live by, I would like to share with you examples of saved mothers and her relationship to her son from the Bible.

In searching the Scriptures, the Biblical examples that I

found after the Day of Pentecost when the Spirit fell, were Salome, the wife of Zebedee's in Matthew 27:56, and Elizabeth, the mother of John the Baptist in Luke 1:57, Also, in II Timothy 1:5, Paul told Timothy that he knew he was faithful because it was first found in his grandmother Lois and also in his mother Eunice. Another Biblical example is Mary, the Mother of Jesus; His birth is recorded in all of the four Gospels. God, in His great love and mercy, allowed Mary his mother to be present for the outpouring of the Holy Spirit.

Tonight, we have gathered to celebrate the accomplishments of the Mothers of the Year for 2013. However, I would like you to allow me the privilege to share with you the story of a Mother that gave up her son many years ago, who will always be remembered as a mother of the year. Mary the mother of Jesus, she is one of the most famous characters in the Bible. Even people who have never read the Bible have heard about the Mother of Jesus Christ. Luke 2:41- 52 records Mary's relationship with her son as an adolescent. This reflects the time He stayed in the Temple and she had to return to find him, she spoke to Him, However, his father Joseph did not say anything. Jesus told his Mother that He had to be about His Father's business. Nevertheless, He was obedient and returned with the family and stated with his Mother until He became 30 years of age.

John 2:1-11 records the first event in the public ministry of Jesus shows the relationship between Him and His Mother at a wedding in Cana of Galilee. She did not tell Him what to do, all she said to Him was, and "They have no wine." But she did tell the servants whatsoever He saith unto you, do it."

Another relationship with her son is when; these words were spoken at the foot of the Cross-,

WOMAN, BEHOLD THY SON! SON BEHOLDS THY MOTHER! They are recorded in Luke 19:26-27. The culture at the time of Jesus' death was the oldest son would have been required to take care of his mother once the father died. Joseph was already dead at this time, and Jesus being the son of Mary was giving her over to John's care.

The term woman here refers to the prophecy in Genesis where the offspring of the woman would crush the serpent's head, which Jesus did with His crucifixion and resurrection. A woman was chosen as the one through whom the Word would be made flesh to dwell among us on earth. The seed of the woman, our Lord and Savior, bruised the head of the serpent.

In Genesis 3:15 these words are recorded "I will put enmity between you and the woman, and between your offspring and hers. He will crush your head, and you will strike his heel." The woman meant here is Eve, the wife of Adam, not Mary. All of humankind descended from Eve. Every human being is an offspring of a woman. However, the special offspring referred to here that would crush the serpent head (meaning "sin") was Jesus. It was only because Jesus was born of Mary, *"born of a woman,"* that He was able to fulfill these words.

Galatians 4:4-5 states "But when the time had fully come, God sent His Son, born of a woman, born under law, to redeem those under law that we might receive the full rights of sons." "Beloved, now are we the sons of God, and it doth not yet appear what we shall be: but we know that, when He shall appear, we shall be like Him; and shall see Him as he is." Every man that hath this hope in him purifies himself, even as He is pure.

These words are recorded in Roman 8:16-17 "The Spirit itself beareth witness with our spirit, that we are the children of God: And if children, then heirs; heirs of God, and join-heirs with Christ; if so be that we suffer with Him, that we may be also glorified together."

The Scripture clearly teaches that the saved mother is obligated to train her son to know and obey God. This is the basis for pleasing Him and living victoriously in His grace. Solomon's advice to the saved mother in Proverbs 22:6 is to "train a child in the way he should go, and when he is old he will not turn from it."

To a saved mother, rearing and training a son within the context of this proverb means that it begins with the Bible. For example, II Timothy 3:16 tells us "all Scripture is God-breathed and is useful for teaching, rebuking, correcting and training." Additionally, II Timothy 3:15 states that teaching sons the truths of Scripture will make them wise for salvation; thoroughly equip them to do good works is found in (2 Timothy 3:17). 1 Peter 3:15 instruct us to "prepare them to give an answer to everyone who asks them the reason for their hope." Mothers must prepare their offspring to withstand the onslaught of cultures bent on indoctrinating them with secular values. In Psalm 127:3, the Bible tells us that sons are a reward from God. It would certainly seem fitting then, that we heed Solomon's wise counsel to train them appropriately.

The saved mother should have a zeal for teaching their sons. We have been given the privilege of being stewards of our son's lives for a very short time, Mary had less than 35 years with her son, but the teaching and training we provide is eternal. According to the promise of Proverbs, a son who is diligently trained in the "way he should go" will remain true to that way in this life and reap its rewards in the next.

Maybe it was only after Mary received the fullness of the Holy Spirit at Pentecost, following Jesus' death and resurrection, that Mary had some of her "whys" answered. Yet she submitted to God's will for her life. She suffered much pain while living through the many things she did not understand. Her son practically ignored her doing His ministry; He did not even call her Mother, Instead, he referred to her as Woman. The Bible does not tell us when or where Mary died. Church tradition records that John took her with him to Ephesus and she was buried there.

We now have Jesus, God's written Word, and the gift of the Holy Spirit to help us understand God's Word to us. However, to receive revelation, we must, like Mary, mediate upon what He has said, and ponder His teachings in our hearts. This takes time, discipline, quietness, expectation, and sensitivity to the Holy Spirit. The results may be conviction of sin, need for intercession, desire to sing praise, or a deepening commitment to the Lord. True meditation creates within us a response toward God, which we must obey in light of what we have received.

A Saved Mother must have a relationship with the son, the King of Kings. Therefore, tonight I would like to ask you some questions to make sure that you know who the King of Kings is. The Bible says my King is the King of the Jews. He's the King of Israel. He's the King of Righteousness. He's the King of the Ages. He's the King of Heaven. He's the King of Glory. He's the King of kings, and He's the Lord of lords. That's my King. I wonder, do you know Him?

My King is a sovereign King. No means of measure can define His limitless love. He's enduringly strong. He's entirely sincere. He's eternally steadfast. He's immortally graceful. He's superiorly powerful. He's shows outstanding mercy. Do you know Him? He's the greatest person that has ever crossed the horizon of this world. He's God's Son. He's the sinner's Savior. He's the centerpiece of civilization. He is the highest idea in literature. He's the highest
204

personality in philosophy. He's the fundamental doctrine of true theology. He's the only one qualified to be an all-sufficient Savior. I wonder if you know Him tonight?

He supplies strength for the weak. He's available for the tempted and the tried. He sympathizes and He saves. He strengthens and sustains. He guards and He guides. He heals the sick. He cleanses the lepers. He forgives sinners. He discharges debtors. He delivers the captive. He defends the feeble. He blesses the young. He serves the unfortunate. He regards the aged. He rewards the diligent. And, He beautifies the meek. I wonder if you know Him?

He's the key to knowledge. He's the wellspring of wisdom. He's the doorway of deliverance. He's the pathway of peace. He's the roadway of righteousness. He's the highway of holiness. He's the gateway of glory. Do you know Him? Well... His life is matchless. His goodness is limitless. His mercy is everlasting. His love never changes. His Word is enough. His grace is sufficient. His reign is righteous. And, His yoke is easy. His burden is light. I wish I could describe Him to you. Yes,...He's indescribable! He's incomprehensible. He's invincible. He's irresistible. You can't get Him out of your mind. You can't get Him off your hand. You can't outlive Him, and you can't live without Him. The Pharisees couldn't stand Him, but they found out they couldn't stop Him. Pilate couldn't find any fault in Him. Herod couldn't kill Him. Death couldn't handle Him, and the grave couldn't hold Him. Yes! That's my King, that's my King. Do you know Him? Mothers, you must know Him in order to have a relationship with the Son. AMEN!! AMEN!!! AMEN!![2]

---

[2] Excerpts from "That's My King" by Dr. S. M. Lockridge.

"Killing" the fatted calf is the setting forth of Christ crucified, preaching the cross and proclaiming the Gospel."

Tonight we are here at this banquet celebrating our Annual Mother of the Year Contest. Women from all over Florida will compete for this title. The one that represents with the highest amount of finance, will be crowed the "Mother of the Year." I want to talk to you about another banquet, a banquet thrown by God almighty to celebrate the salvation of sinners. If I could select a text, it would be found in Luke 15:23 **"And bring hither the fatted calf, and kill it; and let us eat, and be merry."** My subject would be: *"Killing" the fatted calf is the setting forth of Christ crucified, preaching the cross and proclaiming the Gospel."* Say within yourself: **"The fatted calf has been killed, the table is spread, and I am ready to dine with the Master."**

In the Word of God, "fat" things refer to the richest, best, most satisfying, most delightful things. The fattest is the best, the choicest, the most excellent thing. The blessings of God are always referred to as "fat things." In order for us to grasp the message of this parable, (earthly story with a heavenly meaning), we ought to bear in mind the thing which inspired it. If you want to know the meaning and message of any portion of Scripture, always read it and interpret it in its context. The Bible was written to the Jew, Gentiles, and the Church of God and it must be rightly divided. The words of this text was a parable given in response to the haughty, self- righteous snobbery of the Pharisees, who question the fact that the Lord Jesus Christ who is God received sinners and ate with them.

First was the parable of the lost sheep. The second was the lost coin, and the last one that I will be dealing with

206

was the lost son. These parables were our Lord's way of saying, -- "I do, indeed, receive sinners, and eat with them." Our Lord came to seek and saved sinners. The Pharisees' reproach is our Savior's glory and our souls' everlasting joy.

To get a fatted calf, the farmer, will take a calf and put it in a special made pin (area) away from the other cattle. That calf is fed a special diet from the others, a more healthy diet. By eating a healthy diet, all of the bad cells, blood, bones density, and muscles became good. From the day that calf is put into that pin, he knows that the reason he was set aside is in preparation to die!

The fatted calf, of course, represents the Lord Jesus Christ, our crucified Savior. The Lord Jesus here describes Himself by referring to the calves offered in sacrifice, which were offered for sin offerings, and for peace offerings, and for burnt offerings; and were one of the sacrifices on the Day of Atonement. The Lord God has furnished a table, spread with fat things; rich, soul- satisfying food. He bids us to feast with Him in His house. Christ is the best that God can give, and the best we can desire. He is the true manna. He is real Bread, the Bread of life. He nourishes our souls. He is sweet and satisfying. This Bread gives life and preserves it. This Bread nourishes, strengthens, refreshes, delights, and fattens.

On this Christian journey, it is our business, privilege, and responsibility to bring forth the fatted calf and kill it; to preach Christ crucified. We must share Christ with others through the scriptures. We must present Him before all with clarity and simplicity, bidding all to feed upon Him.

The Father Himself says through His servants, "Let us eat and be merry!" This is a wide, far reaching invitation and encouragement to eat of the fatted calf. The people called upon to eat were the Father, the servants, and the returned son. **The Father** is set before us as one to whom the salvation of His people, by the death of Christ, is a feast. This is where God meets men and communes with them! This feast of grace is the great glory of the church. He is the greatest blessing on earth. He is a foretaste of heaven. **The Servants** represent Gospel preachers. God's servants also eat and live upon a crucified Christ. **The Returned Son** – Saved sinners are those for who the Gospel feast is primarily and specifically spread. It is true; the feast is spread before all. However, it is spread specifically for you who are hungry, for you who long to feed upon Christ.

It is recorded in John 6:53-58 "Then Jesus said unto them, verily, verily, I say unto you, except ye eat the flesh of the Son of man, and drink his blood, ye have no life in you. Whoso eateth my flesh, and drinketh my blood, hath eternal life; and I will raise him up a t the last day. For my flesh is meat indeed, and my blood is drink indeed. He that eateth my flesh, and drinketh my blood, dwelleth in me, and I in him. As the living Father hath sent me, and I live by the Father; so he that eateth me, even he shall live by me. This is that bread which came down from heaven: not as your fathers did ear manna, and are dead: he that eateth of this bread shall live forever."

Are you hungry? - Come and dine! - The feast is spread for us! Let us eat with joy! Let us share the joy of faith. The cause of our happiness is God's free, sovereign, saving mercy in Christ. In this parable, the Father began to be merry, the restored son began to be merry, and all the Father's servants began to be merry. In essence, everyone in the Father's house began to be merry, except the older son who represents the self-righteous scribes and Pharisees to whom the parable was addressed. There is a banquet in heaven every time a sinner repents.

Luke 14:23 "And the Lord said unto the servant, Go out into the highways and hedges, and compel them to come in, that my house may be filled."

**"Come and dine," the
Master calleth, "Come
and dine"; You may
feast at Jesus' table
all the time;
He Who fed the
multitude, turned the
water into wine, To
the hungry calleth
now, "Come and
dine."**

Jesus has a table spread Where the saints of God are fed,
He invites His chosen people, "Come, and dine";
With His manna, He doth feed and supplies our every need:
Oh, 'tis sweet to sup with Jesus all the time!

*The disciples came to land, Thus obeying Christ's
command, For the Master called unto them, "Come
and dine"; There they found their heart's desire,
Bread and fish upon the fire; Thus He satisfies the
hungry every time.*

*Soon the Lamb will take His bride To be ever at His
side, All the host of heaven will assembled be; Oh,
'twill be a glorious sight,*

*All the saints in spotless white; And with Jesus
we will feast eternally.*

*"Come and dine," the Master calleth, "Come and
dine"; You may feast at Jesus' table all the time;*

*He Who fed the multitude, turned the water into
wine, To the hungry calleth now, "Come and dine."*

**THE FATTED CALF WAS KILLED, BUT HE IS NOW
ALIVE. HE WAS LOST, AND IS FOUND!!! FOUND
BY THE FATHER'S ELECTING LOVE. FOUND BY
THE SON'S REDEEMING BLOOD. FOUND BY THE
SPIRIT'S IRRESISTIBLE GRACE.**

CHAPTER TWENTY-FIVE

IT'S GOOD TO KNOW THE WORD OF GOD BUT IT IS BETTER TO HEAR AND RECOGNIZE THE VOICE OF GOD

"My sheep hear my voice, and I know them, and they follow me. And I give unto them eternal life; and they shall never perish, Neither shall any man pluck them out of my hand."
John 10:27, 28

When the word BETTER is used, it makes a comparison of two words and that's why "er" is used at the end of the word. Small(er), bett(er) and big(er). The words BEST is used with three or more words are listed and that's when you use "est". Small(est), Best, Big(est). In applying this knowledge, my subject for today is "IT IS GOOD TO KNOW THE WORD – BUT – IT IS "BETTER" TO HEAR AND KNOW THE VOICE OF GOD" Comparing "**knowing the word** with "recognizing the voice of God."

We are Word people and are part of a Word church and are fully persuaded that we must know the Word and be able to rightly divide it, believing that Heaven and Earth will pass away but His Word will stand forever. When we know and recognize the Voice of God, we are in His Hands and no one can pry or snatch us out.

YES, IT IS GOOD TO KNOW THE WORD, BUT IT IS BETTER TO HEAR AND KNOW THE VOICE OF GOD!!!!

How can we recognize the Voice of God? This question has been asked by countless people throughout the ages. Samuel heard the Voice of God, but did not recognize it until he was instructed by Eli (1 Samuel 3:1-10). Gideon had a physical revelation from God, and still doubted what he had

211

heard to the point of asking for a sign; not once, but three times (Judges 6:17-22; 36-40).   When we are listening for God's Voice, how can we know that HE is the one speaking?

First, we have something that Gideon and Samuel didn't have. We have the complete Bible, the inspired Word of God, which we can meditate on,   read, and study.   *"All Scripture is God-breathed and is useful for teaching, rebuking, correcting and training in righteousness, so that the man of God may be thoroughly equipped for every good work"* (II Timothy 3:16-17). When we have a question about a certain topic or decision in our lives, we should see what the Bible has to say about it. God will never lead us or direct us contrary to what He has taught or promised in His Word (Titus 1:2).

Second, In order to hear God's Voice, we must recognize it. Jesus said, *"My Sheep hear my voice, and I know them, and they follow me, and I give eternal life to them, and they will never perish, and no one will snatch them out of my hand. My father, who has given them to me, is greater than all, and no one is able to snatch them out of the Father's hand"* (John 10:27-29). He is saying, My sheep (the believers) listen to My Voice, I know them, and they follow Me. Those who hear God's Voice are those who belong to Him—those who have been saved by His Grace through faith in the Lord Jesus. These are the sheep that hear and recognize His Voice, because they know Him as their Shepherd and they know His Voice. If we are to recognize God's Voice, we must belong to Him.

IT IS GOOD TO KNOW THE WORD, BUT BETTER TO HEAR AND RECOGNIZE GOD'S VOICE.

Third we hear His Voice when we spend time in prayer, Bible study, and quiet contemplation of His Word.

The more time we spend intimately with God and His Word, the easier it is to recognize His Voice and His leading in our lives.

Employees at a bank are trained to recognize counterfeit currency by studying genuine money so closely that it is easy to spot a fake. We should be so familiar with God's Word that when God does speak to us or lead us, it is clear that it is God. God speaks to us so that we may understand the truth. While God can speak audibly to people, He speaks primarily through His Word, and sometimes through the Holy Spirit to our consciences, through circumstances, and through other people. By applying what we hear to the Truth of Scripture, we can learn to recognize His Voice.

Those who are of God hear God's words: (John 8:47)

Jesus cries out seven times to the Seven Churches mentioned in the book of Revelation, *He who has an ear, let him hear what the Spirit says to the churches."* The Holy Spirit is speaking to God's people. Those who listen and obey, are about to move forward into the greatest outpouring of God's Spirit that the world has ever known. *But this is what I commanded them, saying, 'Obey My voice, and I will be your God, and you shall be My people. And walk in all the ways that I have commanded you that it may be well with you. "Yet they did not obey or incline their ear, but followed the counsels and the dictates of their evil hearts, and went backward and not forward* (Jeremiah 7:23-24 NKJV).

As we stand at the edge of the horizon of God's Glory being revealed upon the earth, the greatest need continues to be workers in the harvest. It is through hearing and obeying the Voice of God that we gather the harvest and expand the Kingdom of God. Each believer has a mission and a ministry ordained by God. There is only one head in the Body of Christ, and as we listen and obey His Voice, the Holy Spirit; the Body of Christ will come together in complete unity and function in perfect harmony.

All true believers have heard God's Voice. Jesus says, *"No one can come to Me unless the Father who sent Me draws him; and I will raise him up at the last day. "It is written in the prophets, 'And they shall all be taught by God.' Therefore everyone who has heard and learned from the Father comes to Me.* (John 6:44-45). It was God's Voice that drew you to Him. In your inner most being you heard God saying, *"I have chosen you and ordained you, come unto me."*

We know God's Voice because we know Him. Jesus says, *"I am the good shepherd: I know my sheep and my sheep know me"* (John 10:14 NIV). We recognize God's Voice because we recognize Him and the better we get to know God, the more clearly we will recognize His Voice. God's Voice is His Holy Spirit, the Spirit of Love, so the Voice of God is the sound of Love. The actions of love are accomplished when we put God's benefit and the benefit of others before our own benefit. God's Voice which is the His Holy Spirit will always lead us in the direction of love.

If you feel that God is speaking a message to you but you are not really sure if it is from God here are some good questions to ask yourself about the message:

1. Does it line up with the Holy Bible, the written Scriptures?

2. Does it lead you into a closer relationship with God, a greater unity with Him?

3. Does it lead you into expressing love, which is

putting God's benefit and the benefit of others before your own benefits?

4. Does it lead to a dying of yourself and a greater manifestation of Christ's Life in you?

5. Does it cause greater humility in you, and a greater dependence upon God?

6. Does it cause greater love, joy, and peace from God in you?

BLEST. BROKEN. GIVEN.

CHAPTER TWENTY-SIX

STORY OF A BOLD AND COURAGEOUS WOMAN

"Be of good courage, and let us behave valiantly for our people, and for the cities of our God: and let the Lord do that which is good in his sight." I Chronicles 19:13

Abstract
This biblical character analysis paper is about a bold and courageous woman on a mission for Christ. Her name means "beautiful woman." She was one of the loveliest women in the world. You can read about this woman in the last book of History in the Bible. Her husband was the King who reigned from India even unto Ethiopia over 127 provinces. During his third year of reign he had a party to show off his wealth to his friends which it took 180 days—6 months—1/2 of a year. After 180 days of drunkenness this woman's husband had another party and on the seventh day, he told his servants to bring the woman, his wife to him, the bold, courageous woman – Queen Vashti. The beautiful Queen Vashti, the wife of King Ahasuerus, did not respond to her husband's request. This act publicly humiliated the king was he was advised to answer accordingly. Vashti is seen as a strong character that did not use her beauty to advance her. Queen Vashti is one of the great debates. How her life ended is unknown, but how her Queen ship ended is well-known. There may be times when one has to make the choice of which to obey man or God. There must be some Vashti women in order to make room for the Esther women.

Introduction

The book of Esther holds a high place in the sacred literature of the Jews; although, it has no mention of God or of the Holy Land and contains no definite religious teaching—we don't even know who wrote this book but in this Purim story one will find a bold courageous woman, none other than Esther.

Queen Vashti was the daughter of Belshazzar, the great-granddaughter of King Nebuchadnezzar. By birth she was born a Persian Princess. Her name originates from the Persian words for beautiful woman. During Vashti's father's kingship, he was murdered and Belshazzar's palace was looted. Vashti did not know her father had been killed; she ran to her father's quarters and was captured by Darius who took pity on her and gave the young Princess Vashti to his son Ahasuerus to marry.

The book of Esther records that in the city of Shushan, during Ahasuerus' reign, he had two celebrations prepared to show all his princes and his servants; the power of Persia and Media, the nobles and princes of the provinces. The first festival, for his nobles and princes, lasted for 180 days. The second feast, which ended with a weeklong drinking feast, was for the people, both great and small. During this time Queen Vashti also made a feast for the women.

Esther 1:11-12 (KJV) states, *"To bring Vashti the queen before the king with the crown royal, to shew the people and the princes her beauty: for she was fair to look on. But the queen Vashti refused to come at the king's commandment by his chamberlains: therefore were the king very worth, and his anger burned in him."*

This Queenly woman accepted disgrace and dismissal because she refused to exhibit herself, even at the king's command. She refused to do what was wrong— when she knew what was right. Some commentaries state that the

218

King wants her to wear nothing else but the "Royal Crown." So, all those drunken men could see her naked beautiful body. The Bible plainly declares that the King summoned his wife to the feast "*to show-off her beauty.*" In those days it was the custom of the Queen to sit with her husband during a feast, unless the wine ran freely, then a concubine would come and replace the Queen. They had *wine in abundance according to every man's pleasure (1:8).*

It is recorded in Esther 2:1, "*After these things, when the wrath of King Ashasuerus was appeased, he remembered Vashti, and what she had done, and what was decreed against her.*" A Persian Law once made could never be revoked, the King, now sober, and likely regretful of his impulsive action could not reinstate Vashti.

Vashti's character is usually interpreted as that of a villain but Vashti was a heroine in her own right. She had a soul of her own and preserved its integrity. What the King demanded was a surrender of her womanly honor and Vashti, who was neither vain nor wanton, was unwilling to comply.

Summary

This writer believes had the King been sober he would not have considered such a breach of custom for he was aware that Eastern women lived in seclusion and such a request he made in his drunken condition amounted to a gross insult. The Bible doesn't say what happen to Vashti after she lost her title. But this writer would like to believe that she lived a nice life somewhere in the palace without the "Royal Crown," (outward adorning)—remembering she was born a Princess.

It was also the custom during this time that once a woman had been selected to become a Queen; she had to go through a year of preparation and wait for the King to send for her. Some women waited all their life and lived like a widow because the King never sent for them. But they still lived in the big house, with servants and special treatment. Vashti, this bold courageous woman, sacrificed a kingdom rather than to cater to a drunk and exhibit her body.

There is much speculation as to why Queen Vashti refused to come. But read the Scripture; the King was drunk and he wanted to display her beauty in front of himself and his friends. She must have felt degraded. She is not mentioned much more throughout the book of Esther, but her action showed great strength. She chose her dignity over the law and chose to preserve her self-worth over her husband's ego. The King disposed of her as Queen and chose to find a replacement.

A prime example of acceptable disobedience to authority occurred when Peter and some apostles chose to disobey the Priest of the Temple by continuing to teach and preach in the name of Jesus. They chose, instead to obey God. There are examples in the Old Testament of some Hebrews midwives who spared the lives of male babies because they feared God more than the Egyptian rulers. All praise to the heroic Vashti for her decent disobedience. A bold courageous woman!

On a mission for Christ, one must learn to lead, follow, or move out of the way. Today, titles seems so important to some people. Some will choose to live in denial and blindly serve outside of the Lord's Divine Will and gladly accept His Permissible Will. Everyone can't be Esthers; there must be some Vashtis to make room for the Esther women. One must make sure they're coming and not going.

References

Miclaus, C. (2011). Queen *Vashti.*
http://www.buzzle.com/articles/queen-vashti.html

Pelata, A. *Who was Vashti?*
http://judaism.about.com/od/holidays/a/whowasvashti
htm

The Holy Bible (KJV)

BLEST. BROKEN. GIVEN.

CHAPTER TWENTY-SEVEN

HOW CAN A WIDOW AFFECT THE MINISTRY OF HER CHURCH?

"The Lord preserveth the strangers; he relieveth the fatherless and widows: but the way of the wicked he turneth upside down."

Psalm 146: 9

PURPOSE OF WORKSHOP

- To cause women who no longer have the responsibility of being wives of Ministers or Deacons to examine themselves. Sixty Two percent of the females in the church are single.

- To instruct and motivate women to reach their fullest potential.

- To help participants realize that they are now free to be themselves, to be healthy, and to find their place in the ministry.

- To help women understand more clearly the will of God in their lives when a loved one dies or leaves them and.

- To stimulate a proper attitude among women towards dying, death, grief, and bereavement.

This workshop is designed to be useful both to those who have experienced bereavement and to others who want to be enlightened concerning their attitudes before personal grief is experienced.

SCRIPTURES

*"Remember ye not the former things, neither consider the things of old. Behold, I will do a **NEW** thing, **NOW** it shall spring forth; t know it? I will even make a way in the wilderness and rivers in the desert"* (Isaiah 43:18-19).

WIDOWHOOD is a desolate estate: but let the **widows TRUST** in me and **REJOICE** that they have a **GOD** to turn to" (Jeremiah 49:11).

*"Pure religion and undefiled before God and the Father is this, to visit the fatherless and **WIDOWS** in their affliction, and to keep himself unspotted from the world" (James 1:27).*

"But I would not have you be ignorant, brethren, concerning them which are asleep, that we sorrow not even as others which have no hope" (I Thes. 4:13).

"Let not your heart be troubled, neither let it be afraid" (John 14:17).

AIM: To show Women of God without Spouses how to be healthy in the Ministry. Spiritual health means that one is alive and vibrant in Christ. For that, one needs discipline to help them stay on the right track. One must remain focused on God and not on one's own problems or distractions.

OBJECTIVE: To help these Women of God discover, develop and exercise their gifts in appropriate ministries so that the Body of Christ "grows and builds itself up in love." Remember, Christ is the Head; widows are included in the Body and all else is under feet. *"And the God of peace shall bruise Satan under your feet shortly. The grace of our Lord Jesus Christ be with you."* (Romans 16:20).

APPLICATION: To teach Women of God that effective ministry flows out of a passionate spirituality. Spiritual intimacy leads to a strong conviction that God will act in powerful ways. A Godly vision can only be accomplished through an optimistic faith which views obstacles as opportunities and turns defeats into victories.

"Learn to do well; seek judgment, relieve the oppressed; judge the fatherless, plead for the widow" (Isaiah 1:17).

INTRODUCTION

WIDOWHOOD is a desolate estate, but let the widows **TRUST** in me and **REJOICE** that they have a GOD to turn to (Jeremiah 49:11). The word "hood" means a covering for the head and neck. As a suffix it can mean: A state of being or all the persons or things that are in this state. Widowhood is one earthly covering after the death of one's spouse, as long as she remains unmarried.

The Scriptures have much to say about WIDOWS. In the early Church, one of the first major problems to which the apostles had to give attention was the need of *"those widows who were neglected in the daily administration"* (Acts 6:1). In Ruth 1:20-21, a widow named Naomi cried out to El Shaddai, the "God of More Than Enough", to change her situation from empty bitterness to fullness.

Naomi even changed her name to Mara, which means bitterness. But she never gave up on the idea of trusting in God.

It was a widow who was commanded by God to feed Elijah. Elijah gave the widow instructions. He told her to go home and first make him a cake of bread and bring it to him. Elijah specifically told the widow not to be afraid, for her jar of oil (the **Healing** Power of Jesus) would not be used up until the day of the Lord sent rain on the land. Another moving incident concerning a widow was spoken of by Jesus of the woman who cast into the treasury "two mites," for she *"hath cast in more than them all – that entire she had."*

This workshop will remind the widows to gird themselves with God's Truth and Strength. He will provide a pathway to a healthy, effective life that is perfected in Him. The widow will not be moved, nor will she slip because the Lord will hold her up with His right hand. His gentleness will make her great in overcoming the enemy of death. The Lord will protect the widow and hide her within the secret place under His wing. The widow will overcome the enemy with righteousness, peace, protection, and the Salvation of Jesus Christ. When the enemies such as fear, loneliness, depression, and doubt threaten to overcome her, she must know that the Lord will deliver her and lifted her up above these negative destructive calamities.

SUMMARY

The average age of widowhood in the United States is fifty-six. As a result, half of all women over sixty-five live as widows. This high rate of widowhood occurs because women tend to marry men older than themselves. Also, life expectancy is seven to nine years longer for women than for men. Becoming a widow often means that a relationship lasting most of a lifetime has ended; it can cause profound grief. Furthermore, recovery is often painful and takes time. The period of most intense grief can last from a few months to a year or more.

During this time, it is normal for women to feel despair or depression, irritability, and even anger toward the person who died. The fact that she cries or talks a great deal about him is also normal until she finally accepts his death. After the grieving process, a woman is usually able to increase her range of independence and find new friends and activities to enrich her life. Some women need special help with the social and psychological problems associated with being widowed.

Loneliness is also common during this period. It sometimes takes an extra effort to find social activities and friends, but many resources are available. Many women make new friendships through a variety of affiliations with religious, civic, or volunteer organizations, and through community and social activities.

Women who find themselves alone as a result of being widowed may need to develop new skills for a changing role. For example, some must learn to manage financial matters for the first time – such as paying bills, balancing a checkbook, and handling insurance benefits. To help them, a growing number of national and local organizations provide support. God can take widows, when their world has been turned upside down by loss, grief and sorrow; and turn each life *"right side up"* through biblical wisdom.

There are three essential characteristics of the believer (**Widow**) to apply so the Father will be able to pursue their heart's cry:

    1. **RISK** – Begin to be stretched, widow. Stand in the gap of risk. God will move you out in His strength according to the greatness of your need. WALK BY FAITH.

2. **TRUST** – As God stretches you. He will pour more of Himself into you, one step at a time. Step out of the boat and walk on God's Word toward your dream.

3. **KNOW THE SOURCE OF YOUR DREAM AND VISION** – Make sure you have a close relationship with the Lord, especially during a crisis. Allow each crisis to push you closer to the Lord. Spend time with Him daily. Have an intimate relationship with Him. Let the Lord reveal Himself to you. He is truly new every morning.

SINGLE AGAIN

The widow must become a "New" person in Christ Jesus, who is filled with God's wisdom. She is able to overcome the grief and sorrow with God's Word. Heaven is counting on the widow. God created everything with *potential,* including the widow.

Potential is not what one has done, but what one is yet able to do. It is important that the widows never let what they cannot do interfere with what they can do. The greatest tragedy in life is not death, but life that never realized its full potential. The widows must decide today not to rob the world of the rich, valuable, potent, untapped resources locked away within themselves. Potential never has a retirement plan.

SELF is the biggest obstacle widow will face and this is due to the lack of confidence following the loss of her spouse.

During this session, the widow can claim <u>victory</u> by the renewal of her mind. The mind is where emotions are— the actions and reaction to circumstances in life. The widow is now free to be herself and pursue those things that will now be fulfilling. To be a total woman in Christ means stepping out of one's shell and being restored. It is time for the widow to reach out with clean hands and a pure heart. She must remember this is not the end, but just the beginning.

The Lord is near to those (widows) who have a broken heart, and saves such as have a contrite spirit. Many are the *afflictions* of the righteous, but the Lord delivers His (**widows**) out of them all… ***"The Lord redeems the soul of His servants, and none of those who <u>trust</u> Him shall be desolate"*** **(Psalms 34:18-19, 22).** When the Lord offers His outstretched hand to guide you, Dear Widows, let Jesus' fingertips touch your fingertips.

> *"Though I walk in the midst of trouble, thou wilt revive me; thou shalt stretch forth thine hand against the wrath of mine enemies, and thy right hand shall save me"* (Psalms 138:7).

The beginning of *"personhood"* is change.   Let the widows admit they have a broken personality and allow the Lord to mend the hurting parts to completeness again. The starting point of your destination is self—personhood. Widows should receive God's instruction, knowledge, and counsel; find favor, strength, and a renewed life in Christ.

TEN STEPS FOR THE WIDOW TO AFFIRM PERSONHOOD TO BE HEALTHY AND FIND HER PLACE IN MINISTRY

1. **MAKE GOD'S WILL THE NUMBER ONE PRIORITY IN YOUR LIFE.**

   "Trust in the Lord with all thine heart, and lean not unto thine own understanding" (Proverbs 3:5).

2. **LET GOD BE YOUR SOURCE OF SECURITY AND STABILITY.**

   "For the king trusteth in the Lord, and through the mercy of the most High He shall not be moved" (Psalms 21:7).

3. **LET GOD PERFORM AND ACCOMPLISH ALL THINGS.**

   "I will cry unto God most high; unto God that performeth all things for me" (Psalms 57:2).

4. **LET JESUS BE YOUR REDEEMER.** *Then they remembered that God was their (widow's) rock, and the Highest God their redeemer* (Psalms 78:35).

5. **HAVE A SECRET HIDING PLACE IN GOD.** *(Widows) who dwell in the secret place of the Most High shall abide under the shadow of the almighty* (Psalms 91:1).

6. **HAVE THE MIND OF CHRIST.** *"Let this mind be in you which was also in Christ Jesus"* (Philippians 2:5).

7. **LET CHRIST BE THE HEAD OF YOUR LIFE.** *And He has put all things under His feet, and gave Him to be head over all widows* (Ephesians 1:22).

8. **BE CONSISTENT IN YOUR FAITH**. Widows, do not grow weary; consistency is like a golden thread that weaves your life back together, and it is a battle worth winning. *And let us not be weary in well doing: for in due season we (widows) shall reap, if we faint not* (Galatians 6:9).

9. **IMITATE GOD HIMSELF BY TAKING TIME FOR LEISURE**.
The Lord made the Heavens and the earth, and on the seventh day He rested and was refreshed (Exodus 31:17) REST!

10. **GET SUPPORT FROM OTHER PEOPLE AND LET THEM ENTER INTO THE LONELY EXPERIENCE WITH YOU.** Do not endure stress alone. But select capable saved friends that will make your load lighter by sharing it with them (Exodus 18:21, 22).

Widows, when you are lonely you need an understanding friend – JESUS. You need strength to keep putting one foot in front of the other—Jesus is your strength. Love the Lord your God with all your heart, soul, mind, and with all your strength. God wants your arms around Him and wants to hear you tell Him that you <u>love</u> and <u>trust</u> Him.

TOP 10 WAYS A WIDOW CAN BOOST SPIRITUAL HEALTH

Faith is a tremendous gift from God. But it takes some extra effort in the midst of the widow's busy lives to stay spiritually healthy. Many things compete for her attention. The widow must yearn to know God more deeply, but her lifestyle choices often make it next to impossible. Then she wonders why she feels spiritually empty, dried up, even sick. Widows should embrace grace and practice what they believe.

There is no standardized list of prescribed spiritual practices, but here are ten disciplines, or habits, (not in any particular order) that many widows throughout the centuries have found helpful in boosting their spiritual health:

1. *Prayer; silence and solitude:* Spending time in God's presence, with or without words, empowers the widows. It is a privilege and a gift to be able to commune with God through prayer.

2. *Listening to God; spiritual journaling:* Listening, paying attention to God's whisper in the widows' heart reminds them that God is active in their lives. Writing down prayers, thoughts, questions, longings and hopes proves meaningful to many widows of faith.

3. *Private and corporate worship:* Praising God opens the widows to the Holy Spirit, reorders their priorities and redirects their paths. Worship connects widows to God on a holistic level.

4. *Bible-reading and study:* Meditating on God's Word keeps the widows focused on God, rather

than or their problems and wants. God speaks to them through the Bible and **personally guides them.**

5. *Obeying God's commands:* Putting the widows' faith into practice increases their joy. This is one of the paradoxes of faith; when widows submit themselves to God, they find themselves, and in an odd way, they are freed.

6. *Loving God and our neighbors:* Surrendering to God leads widows to a life of love. God is love, and when widows live and serve in Christ, they experience love themselves.

7. *Stepping out in faith when urged to do something:* Trusting in God's guidance strengthens widows' faith. When they dare to step out in faith, they learn that God is with them wherever they go and that God is more powerful than their fear.

8. *Fasting, not necessarily from food-perhaps from* television *or something else:* Finding time or space to pay attention to God by giving up something else blesses widows beyond measure. They need to guard their hearts as well as their time from distractions.

9. *Serving others:* Reorienting their attitude away from self keeps widows on the right track. Following Jesus in serving others heightens their own experience of grace.

10. *Fellowship with other believers:* Building and being part of a ministry equips widows for sharing and caring, within and beyond the Church building. The values of God's kingdom are different than those of the world, so widows need the support and encouragement of other believers in order to truly live as saints in their daily lives.

It is important to remember that disciplines are not ends in themselves, but means to the end of <u>not</u> knowing God more deeply. When the widows seek God, they will find Him because He wants to be found. The widows cannot earn salvation—they are saved through faith by grace (Romans 3:24-25) - but they can make the effort to stay spiritually healthy. When they are full alive in Christ, they are also robust in spiritual health.

ADDITIONAL WAYS TO HELP IMPROVE SPIRITUAL HEALTH:

- Be Quiet. Take time for yourself every day, even if it's just before you go to sleep, or when you're driving home.
- Be Open. Spiritual experiences can happen anywhere at any time.
- Practice being non-judgmental and having an open mind.
- Be receptive to pain or times of sorrow. It is often in these times when widows discover how spirituality can help them cope.
- Practice forgiveness.
- Pray, meditate and worship.
- Live joyfully.
- The widows must allow themselves to believe in things that cannot easily be explained.

THINGS A WIDOW CAN DO TO BE PART OF A HEALTHY LAITY HOW CAN SHE AFFECT THE MINISTRY OF HER CHURCH

Get her home and family in order, according to God's Word and Jesus' character. Free her home from pride, selfishness, hatred and impurity. Make sure her home has the atmosphere that will be inviting for Jesus to bring in love, grace and guidance. Let the Holy Spirit dwell in her home to strengthen and comfort her in her time of weakness. Jesus will be there beside her as she moves along her journey according to a divinely planned "road map" toward eternity and her eternal home. Travel in PEACE and with the GRACE of God as her constant traveling companion.

The Holy Spirit gives to every saint spiritual gift(s) for the building of God's Kingdom. church leaders have the responsibility to help believers discover, develop and exercise their gifts in appropriate ministries so that the Body of Christ" grows and builds itself up in love."

The Church is the living Body of Christ. Like all healthy organisms, it requires numerous systems which work together to fulfill its intended purpose. Each must be evaluated regularly to determine if it is still the best way to accomplish the intended purpose.

Inspiring worship is a personal and corporate encounter with the living God. Both personal and corporate worship must be infused with the presence of God resulting in times of joyous exultation and times of quiet reverence. Inspiring worship is not driven by particular style or ministry focus group, but rather the shared experience of God's awesome presence.

Loving relationships are the heart of a healthy, growing church. Jesus said people will know we are His disciples by our love. Practical demonstration of love builds authentic widows and brings others into God's Kingdom. Healthy organisms do not grow endlessly, but reproduce themselves. *"Learn to do well; seek judgment; relieve the oppressed; judge the fatherless and plead for the widows"* (Isaiah 1:17).

CONCLUSION

What makes the _laity_ healthy or unhealthy? This comes from a big problem that is in most churches today, that is tendency of leaders not effectually growing in the Lord and thus do not practice their faith. This dispenses down to the congregation. The outcome is a church that has missed its point and reason for being. The people whom Christ brought in, go without being taught or disciplined. Being healthy means one knows not just Who Christ is, but realize that His impact has gone deep and has occupied al l aspects of one 's li f e and faith. Life is all about Him and not about selfish ideas or perceptions.

The believers have gone to His throne and His priestly duty has been received, His Milk, the feast upon the Meat, then His wondrous Precepts and Truth are manifested. So one's faith is real, personal, fully transformed and that person becomes fully engaged followers of Christ seen by a life well lived. If one wants to be an impacting lay leader in a church that impacts its community and world, one has to eat the meat of God's precepts with passion and conviction, in love and in truth and then share with others.

The LAITY that is healthy is in line with and in touch with Jesus Christ as Savior and Lord. The leaders and the people have an effectual sense of God's presence and seek Him out of gratitude for who He is and what He has done. Their growing faith and their joyful attitude in life will evidence this.

"The Lord is my shepherd; I shall not want" (Psalm 23:1). No other Old Testament words have brought more comfort to souls in distress than this Shepherd Psalms. Millions have had their faith strengthened through Paul's great Resurrection Chapter, I Corinthians 15. Peter, the Apostle of Hope, has brought encouragement to countless others. John, the Apostle of Love, reveals Him who is the

Light and life of men.

In II Corinthians 4:8-10, Paul testifies at Corinth to the Saints in Achaia. " *"We are troubled on every side, yet not distressed; we are perplexed but not despair, persecuted but not forsaken, cast down, but not destroyed. Always bearing about in the body the dying of the Lord Jesus that the life also of Jesus might be made manifest in our body."* Yes, the widows can see trouble on every side; the United States of America is in a recession, but as the economy decreases the Saints of God actually increase. The widow should not be distressed because she knows that victory is coming her way. The Scripture teaches how the Lord always delivers His children; over and over again and how He can reverse any situation to accomplish His will. The more familiar one becomes with how God worked in the past, the better equipped one is for learning His will for the present and the future.

Yes, widows are perplexed but not in despair. They know that the Lord Himself asked the rhetorical question in Genesis 18:14 *"Is anything too hard for the Lord?"* The widow can always look to the Lord, knowing that His delight is in doing things that seem to be impossible. He always keeps His promises. The widow should never give up on the Lord because He is always on time. Widows can always look to the Lord when they feel that situations are tough and that no one cares. God will always provide; it may not be what they want but what they need.

Remember how to reach the Lord; His address is Post Office Box "PRAISE." He inhabits the praises of the widows.

BLEST. BROKEN. GIVEN.

CHAPTER TWENTY-EIGHT

MARY, THE MOTHER OF JESUS

"And, behold, thou shalt conceive in thy womb, and bring forth a son, and shalt call his name JESUS." Luke 1:31

The first mention of Mary in the Gospels concerns the appearance of an angel:

"In the sixth month God sent the angel to Galilee to a virgin pledged to be married to a man named Joseph, a descendant of David" (Luke 1:26-27).

Luke writes that Joseph was a descendant of David, yet when he records the family tree of Jesus in Luke 3:23-38 he gives the ancestors of Mary, not of Joseph. Mary was also a descendant of David, from David's son, Nathan. Her husband, Joseph descended from David's son, Solomon. The genealogy of Joseph is found in Matthew 1:1-16).

The angel went to her and said: "Greetings, you who are highly favored! The Lord is with you." Mary was greatly troubled at his words and wondered what kind of greeting this might be. But the angel said to her, "Do not be afraid, Mary, you have found favor with God. You will give birth to a Son, and you are to give Him the name Jesus. He will be great and will be called the Son of the Most High. The Lord God will give Him the throne of His father David and He will reign over the house of Jacob forever, His Kingdom will never end." "How will this be," Mary asked, "since I am a virgin?" The angel answered, "The Holy Spirit will come upon you, and the power of the Most High will overshadow you, so the Holy One to be born will be called the Son of God." Even Elizabeth your relative is going to have a child in her old age, and she who was said to be barren is in her sixth month. "For nothing is impossible with God." "I am the Lord's servant," Mary answered, "May it happen to me as you have said." Then the angel left her (Luke 1:28-38).

MARY'S SONG

When Mary heard the words of the angel, she sang a song of praise to God (Luke 1:46-55). There is another song in the Bible like Mary's song. This is the Song of Hannah, the mother of Samuel, which is recorded in I Samuel 2:1-10.

Mary thanked God for helping Israel and remembering to be merciful to Abraham and his descendants. Mary descended from Abraham, as were all the people of Israel and by providing this special child, God was showing his mercy not only to Abraham's descendants but even to Abraham himself. It may sound strange that God could "show His mercy" to Abraham by the birth of Jesus, because he was long dead when Mary sang this song. Mary saw that the Child, Jesus, would be a fulfillment of promises that God had made to Abraham (Galatians 3:3-9; 14).

THE BIRTH OF JESUS

Mary and Joseph lived in the north of Israel, but the prophecies concerning the future King of Israel, "the Messiah", said that the King must be born in the town of Bethlehem, in the south of Israel (see Micah 52 as quoted in Matthew 2:6). In order for the prophecy to be fulfilled God arranged circumstances so that Mary, even though she was heavily pregnant, had to travel to Bethlehem (Luke 2:1-7).

Jesus' birth was the most important birth in history. More than that, the birth, death and resurrection of Jesus form the central point in the purpose God's creation of the world. God had seen so clearly the need for Christ that he is described as "the lamb slain before the foundation of the world" (Revelation 13:8).

BORN OF A WOMAN

It is important to understand and believe that Mary was the literal mother of Jesus. This means one can read the rest of the Gospel records in a simple and literal way. It is also significant because when Jesus was literally born of a woman, it means that he also was human – he was made with certain characteristics common to all men and women. These characteristics which Christ shared with us were essential to his work. *"But when the time had fully come, God sent his Son, born of a woman, born under law, to redeem those under law that we might received the full rights of sons"* (Galatians 4:4-5).

THE SEED OF THE WOMAN

There is another reason why we should think that Jesus did not exist until his mother, Mary, gave birth to him. And that is the curse on the serpent in the garden, of Eden.

"I will put enmity between you and the woman, and between your offspring and hers. He will crush your hear, and you will strike his heel" (Genesis 3:15).

The woman meant here is Eve, the wife of Adam, not Mary. All mankind are descendants of Eve, and are all offspring of women. But the special offspring referred to here who would crush the serpent (meaning "sin", see Psalm 91:13, Luke 10:18) was Jesus. *It was only because Jesus*

*was born of Mary, "born of a woman", that he was able
to fulfill these words. If Jesus had existed in heaven before
he was born, than he would not have been a descendant of
the woman at all – in fact he would have preceded Eve.*

THE BABY JESUS PRESENTED IN THE TEMPLE

Jesus was born in Bethlehem, where He was circumcised, and named. (Luke 2:21) Mary, like all Jewish women after giving birth, had to observe forty days of purification. When this was completed, she and Joseph made the ten kilometer journey to the Temple in Jerusalem to offer the poor person's sacrifice for Jesus: a pair of doves. God had promised that Simeon, the old priest at the temple, would not die until he (Simeon) had seen the Messiah – the Christ. When saw Jesus, he took the baby in his arms and praised God.

"Sovereign Lord, as you have promised, you now dismiss your servant in peace. For my eyes have seen your salvation, which you have prepared in the sight of all people, a light for revelation to the Gentiles and for glory to your people Israel" (Luke 2:20).

Also at the temple, there was a widow, Anna, 84 years old, who was a prophetess.

"Coming up to them at that very moment she gave thanks to God and spoke about the child to all who were looking forward to the redemption of Jerusalem" (Luke 2:38).

CHAPTER TWENTY-NINE

HOW TO MAKE WISE CHOICES AND DECISIONS

"The way of a fool is right in his own eyes: but he that hearkeneth unto counsel is wise" Proverbs 12:15

"And at midnight there was a cry made, Behold, the bridegroom cometh; Go ye out to meet Him." Mathew 25:6

Wake up! Wake up, Sister! The King is coming! Look at your sister, grab and shake her and look into her eyes and say, sister, oh sister, wake-up! The King is coming, get up, and get ready to receive the King. "The marketplace is empty, no more traffic in the street. All the builders' tools are silent, there's no more time to harvest wheat. Busy housewife will you cease your labor? In the courtroom there is no debate; for the trial has been suspended as the King comes through the gate. Oh the King is coming, The King is coming, and I just heard the trumpet sounding, Oh His Face I see. Oh, the King is coming, Oh, the King is coming. Praise the Lord He's coming for me. Hallelujah thank you Jesus."

Wake up! The King is coming, get excited. Sisters we ought to be excited because He is coming to carry us home. It may be morning, night or noon; no one knows the day or the hour. So get right church and let's go home. Home, to a place prepared just for us; for you see that we will move to a brand new home.

We'll have a new name, a new walk and a new talk. We're busy as a Bride adorned for her Bridegroom. So get ready, the King is coming. He's coming, and it won't be long and we'll be leaving here soon. So, you better be

243

ready and make the wise choice and the decision to be READY and not getting ready. Time is winding up, you don't have time to go and buy. Will you be ready when the King gets here?

Now that you know the King is coming, let's see what some people call Him:

- Some call Him Almighty King – *I'm the Almighty God*

- Some call Him the Blood – *It came streaming down for you and me*

- Some call Him Christ – *the Risen Savior*

- Some call Him Deliver – *thou art my help and deliver*

- Some even call Him an Everlasting Father – *His name shall be everlasting Father*

- Still some call Him God - *the Creator of Heaven and Earth*

- Some call Him "I Am" – *I am that I am that sent thee*

- He's called Jehovah Jireh– *the Lord will provide. King of Kings, Lord of Lords, Master, Jehovah Nissi, Omnipotent, Peace.*

He'll be our peace in the midst of a storm. He will Quicken: He'll make you alive in the twinkling of an eye. Redeemer: Let the redeemed of the Lord say so. Son and Savior: The Father sent the Son to be the Savior of the world. Teacher: He will teach you all things. Victory: He will swallow death up in victory. Everybody calls Him worthy: He's worthy to be praised. Worthy is the Lamb that was slain from the foundation of the world. Oh, how excellent is His Name above Heaven and Earth. So, be wise in making your choices and decisions, on what to call Him.

He's coming, I tell you, and He's coming real soon. When the trumpet sounds will you be ready to go into meet the bridegroom? How is the King coming? Surely He is not coming on foot, by car, bus, train nor plane. So, if you're looking for Him to use some modern transportation, then you're looking in vain. Look at how the Scripture says He's coming:

> I Thessalonians 4:16-17 *"For the Lord He shall descend from Heaven with a shout, and the voice of the archangels, and with the trump of God: and the dead in Christ shall rise first: Then we which are alive and remain shall be caught up together with them in the clouds, to meet the Lord in the air: and so shall we ever be with the Lord."*

> Matthew 24:26-27; 29-31 *"Wherefore if they shall say unto you, Behold, he is the desert; go not forth; behold, he is in the secret chambers; believe it not. For as the lightning cometh out of the east, and shineth even unto the west; so shall also the coming of the Son of man be. Immediately after the tribulation of those days shall the sun be darkened,*

> *and the moon shall not give her light, and the stars shall fall from heaven, and the powers of the heavens shall be shaken: And then shall appear the sign of the Son of man in heaven; and then shall all the tribes of the earth mourn, and they shall see the Son of man coming in the clouds of heaven with power and great glory. And he shall send his angels with a great sound of a trumpet, and they shall gather together his elect from*

the four winds, from one end of heaven to the other."

Revelation 1:7 *"Behold, he cometh with clouds; and every eye shall see him, and they also which pierced him; and all kindreds of the earth shall wail because of him. Even so, Amen."*

Revelation 22:12 -13 *"And, behold, I come quickly; and my reward is with me, to give every man according as his work. I am Alpha and Omega, the beginning and the end, the first and the last.""*

It is your choice, so be wise and make the right decisions. Choices come with consequences; sometimes good and sometimes bad. Remember the parable of the ten virgins: five foolish and five wise. Sometimes the choice is not between right and wrong but between good and better. The Lord will reward those who make wise spiritual choices and show steadfast obedience and loyalty. Yet any choice we make will be right one if made with these words of Jesus in mind: *But seek first the Kingdom of God and His righteousness, and all these things shall be added to you"* (*Matthew* 6:33).

He's coming, I tell you, and He'll present it to himself a glorious Church, not having spot, or wrinkle, or any such thing; He's coming for none but the righteous. He is coming for those who have done what Paul said in Romans 12:1-2 present their bodies a living sacrifice, holy, acceptable unto God, which is your reasonable service, and were not conformed to this world, but was transformed by the renewing of their mind.

The fifth Chapter of Matthew states that He is coming for those who are poor in spirit, mourn, meek, hunger and thirst after righteousness sake, are the salt of the earth, the light of the world, and those who've seek first the kingdom of God His righteousness. But that's not all. Jesus is coming for those who've counted the cost and taken up

246

their cross; those who are born again; those who are new creatures in Christ; those who've cried in the midnight hours and wiped the tears from their weeping eyes; and those who've come through great trials and tribulation and washed their robes in the Blood of the Lamb.

He's also coming for those who walk not after the flesh but after the spirit in love, joy, peace, longsuffering, gentleness, goodness, faith, meekness and temperance. He will come for those who confessed with their mouth the Lord Jesus and believed in their heart that God raised Him from the dead. Also, He will come for those who put on the Whole Armor of God and were able to stand against the wiles of the Devil. Jesus is coming for those who stood, had their loins girded about with truth, and have on the breastplate of righteousness. He will come for those whose feet were shod with the preparation of the gospel of peace; those who took the shield of faith and were able to quench all the fiery darts of the wicked. Jesus also will take back with Him, those who took the helmet of salvation and the sword of the spirit, which is the word of God.

Wake up! Wake up! The King is coming. Get excited about His coming and be concerned about those who are not excited. Those who are unrighteous, fornicators, idolaters, adulterers, effeminate, abusers of themselves with mankind, thieves, covetous, drunkards, revilers, extortionist, those who engage in hatred, jealousy, variance, strife, wrath, divisions, heresies, envying and murder.

So, we had better wake up and go tell everybody that the King is coming. Wake up and take them to the Cross of Calvary. He went to Calvary, rose from the grave and He's coming back again. Judas betrayed Him, Peter denied Him, Pilate whipped Him, the mob mocked Him, and He was dragged from the judgment hall to judgment. Simon helped Him, His mother mourned for Him, the solders pierced

Him in His side, out came blood and water. Two thieves were beside Him. Joseph buried Him. But it didn't end there, No! No!

For you see Satan, was dancing and jumping up and down saying, "The King is Dead!" But God was not to be defeated. Jesus stayed in the earth three days: He went down into Hell and set the captives free and took the keys of death and Hell out of Satan's hands. Can't you see Hell was upset and buzzing because the captives were saying, "The King Is Coming and We're Excited? We Need to Wake up, be Excited and Stay Excited, because the King is Coming!"

That's why the market place is empty and there is no more traffic in the street. All the builder's tools are silent there is no more time to harvest wheat. All you busy housewives need to cease your labor. You see in the courtroom, there will be no debate, for the trial has been suspended because the King is coming through the gate.

Oh, the King is coming, the King is coming. Praise God! We can hear the trumpet sounding! We'd better make ready and be a witness, for we have a story to tell and we need to tell it right now, today, like yesterday and forever more. Wakeup the King is coming! This is my story, this is my song, and I'll praise Him all the day long.

We are to be like the Wise Virgins and make the wise choice; one that will provide both temporal and eternal blessings. Make a decision to keep oil in your vessel and your wicks trimmed and burning. Be ready to walk in when the Bridegroom comes for His bride – the Church.

CHAPTER THIRTY

MY HEALING TESTIMONY

"And it shall come to pass, that before they call,
I will answer; and while they are yet speaking, I will hear."
- Isaiah 65:24

During April of 2005 after a week of a pounding in my right ear, I could hear and feel my heart beating in my ears. I sought relief at the Halifax Hospital Emergency Room in Daytona Beach, Florida. I did not tell my family; in fact, they did not know my where about until the hospital called them. After a series of tests and a call to my primary doctor, I was informed that I would be admitted and that my family should be called. All of my children came to the emergency room and I heard the doctor say, "Your Mother has an inoperable tumor in the right front lobe of her brain, and her doctor would like to have her admitted for further tests."

As the doctor was talking, my oldest son kept saying, "I won't accept this." repeatedly. He was drowning out the doctor's voice, until it was hard to hear the physician telling us what the x-ray had revealed. I looked at him because I felt we needed to pay close attention to what the doctor was saying. This why I chose Isaiah 65:24 as the Scripture to begin my personal testimony. I do believe now that as the doctor was speaking, the Lord was hearing and healing.

The doctor said "This is a condition she'll have to live with." Many people have this, and live a normal life. Your Mother is lucky she found it early. It is the size of the point of this pen and there are exercises that she will be trained to do which will stimulate her brain cells. Eventually she will lose her memory and the ability to create."

I instructed my family, not to tell anyone that I was in the hospital because I didn't want the phone calls or visitors. I just wanted to turn myself inside out because I knew that I didn't want to live—without my memory. Of course, they did not honor this request. The State Women's Day convened that Saturday at my local church in Orlando. My daughter explained my absence, my hospitalization and my condition. She said that we needed a miracle. Women from all over the State of Florida prayed, "Before they called, Jesus will answer."

I saw the neurologist on Monday and the first thing out of his mouth was "Who told you, you had a brain tumor?" I shared what the emergency room doctor had said. He said, "I see something on your x-ray and your MRI reveals something but I don't believe it is a tumor. I am going to start you on some strong blood thinner and when you are discharged, call my office for an appointment for a follow up."

For eight days, I went through all sorts of tests. Every day, three to four times a day, I was asked, "What's your name? What's today's date? What are your grandchildren's names? Who's the President of the United States? What's your address? Phone number, etc? I devised a system in my mind that would help me to be able to answer those questions correctly.

I came home wanting to believe and accept my healing, but fear wouldn't allow me to give God the glory. I started living and making preparation for someone who would eventually lose their memory and the ability to create. I came up with ways to cope in this situation.

When I did make the appointment with the neurologist, he still wasn't sure what was wrong with me. He gave me a prescription to help with seizures that he felt would occur as we waited for certain symptoms to develop, and then he would know, what treatment was necessary. His instructions were so complicated, "Start with this amount, then each day decrease to this amount," that I felt I couldn't remember, so I threw the prescription out of the car window on the way home. Then I resolved within myself, if the Lord doesn't heal me, the medicine won't get the glory.

After months of doing anything that I thought would help my brain cells stimulated, i.e. crossword and Sudoku puzzles, television shows, Jeopardy, Wheel of Fortune, Do You Want to be a Millionaire?, writing a book, creating different recipes for cooking tasty dishes, designing T Shirts, or anything that would cause me to think. However, I became bored and wearied of this way of life.

In September of 2005, I enrolled in the W. L. Bonner College in Columbia, South Carolina to study the Word of God for brain stimulation and because I was afraid to be by myself, all day, all the time because I wasn't sure what I would do; I just didn't want to live without my memory. I thought being on sacred grounds would help me to control my overwhelming emotion of fear.

I knew how much my family loved and depended on me but I also realize that I had trained them that when one family member goes down, we all assist and stay with that one to help them recover and then we would all get up together. Whatever state I was in, they would prop me up, encourage me, and if necessary "carry" me, but I couldn't accept this lifestyle for us.

When I first arrived at the W. L. Bonner College, as I prepared for bed, I would put on my finest lingerie, with my robe neatly placed on the foot of the bed. I dressed up, instead of removing anything. I made sure everything was neatly place, preparing the room for Bishop Bonner to come in and pray for me. I soon found out that a lot of the time during the first part of the Institute Week, Bishop Bonner wasn't even on campus. When I arrived early Monday mornings, I would look to see where his car was parked and then I could tell if he was on campus. During the day I was able to cope by staying busy, but the nights were when I was tormented with fear. Because of respiratory problems, I had to sleep with oxygen during the night. Medicare had the tanks delivered to the dormitory.

Before I left WLBC (3 ½ years), I could *laugh at faith* as I "undressed" for a sweet night of sleep. The acquiring of dynamic faith is accomplished by prayer, by reading the Bible and by practicing its faith techniques. The ability to possess and utilize faith must be studied and practiced to gain perfection.

The class *"The Power of Positive Thinking"* taught by Bishop Bonner was what pulled me back to reality. The concept of positive thinking permeated my soul. It is a philosophy of faith that does not ignore life's problems; but rather explains a practical approach to life's full potential. It is a system of creative living based on spiritual techniques, and its operation was demonstrated in my life. These principles have worked so effectively over the past six years that they are now firmly established as documented truth.

Self-confidence leads to self-realization and achievement. In June of 2008, I graduated as Salutatorian from the WLBC with the Bachelor of Religious Studies, with a focus in Women's Ministries. In August of 2011, I completed the online requirements for a Master's of Arts: Theological Studies at Liberty University in Lynchburg, VA. At present, I am enrolled in the Education Specialist (Ed.S.) Educational Leadership Cognate at Liberty University and have completed twelve semester hours, toward a Doctoral Degree.

In the aging process, one's memory will gradually decrease, so at the age of 74 this is a fact of life for me. The Scripture, in Ecclesiastes the 12th chapter, attests to this. I also have developed a selective memory. I don't try to remember my past hurts and wounds. Yes, I believe the wounds are healed but scars where left with scabs that can be rubbed off. Therefore, I have saturated my thoughts with peaceful experiences, peaceful words and ideas. I now have a storehouse of peace-producing experiences to which I can turn for refreshment and renewal of my spirit.

Was I healed of a brain tumor? I can only say like the blind man in John chapter 9, "All I know is that I don't have that pounding in my head anymore." It has been more than seven years since my diagnosis, I have not had any seizures and I still have the activity all of my limbs. I have peace of mind, improved health, and a never-ceasing flow of energy. In short, my life is full of joy and satisfaction. I have the desire to live and I am not afraid anymore. I am living a victorious life! To God be the Glory!

CHAPTER THIRTY-ONE

MOMENTS OF MEDITATION

"Let the words of my mouth, and the meditation of my heart, be acceptable in thy sight, O Lord, my strength, and my redeemer." Psalm 19:14

Scripture Text: II Chronicles 7:14

If my people who are called by my name: This establishes a relationship with the Lord. Although God is the creator of all things, everyone does not belong to Him. If you don't know Jesus in the pardoning of your sins, and haven't accepted Him as your personal Savior, you are not a part of His family, and He does not hear your prayers (John 9:31).

Shall humble themselves: Humility should be part of the Women of God's character. A person who is humble is not one who is full of pride or thinks more highly of herself than she ought (Romans 12:3).

Pray and seek my face: A child of God should always pray (I Thessalonians 5:17). Seeking God's face is where we fall short. We are so busy asking the Lord to bless us, until we forget to ask the Lord how we can bless Him? "Have you ever asked the Lord, "What can I do for you today?" or "Use me to be a witness for you today?" What joy we get in being a servant for the Lord if we would learn to see the Lord first, all other desires would follow (Matthew 6:33).

Turn from your wicked ways: True repentance is more than mere words uttered to the Lord. True repentance demands a willingness to change. If any man be in Christ, He is a new creation: old things are passed away... (II

Corinthians 5:17). In other words, I don't walk, talk, or live the way I used to. Why? Because I'm a new creature. What would happen to our World if God's people would meditate on these things? If we do our part, God promised that He would **hear, forgive, and heal.** The key to answered prayers requires some spiritual conditioning with the body of Christ.

WHAT DOES FAITH MEAN?

FAITH means drawing from an inner source and relying on God.

FAITH means believing you can do all things through Christ who give you strength (Phil. 4:13).

FAITH means the Lord is your Shepherd (Psalm 23:1).

FAITH means the Lord is your light and your salvation (Psalm 27:1).

FAITH means the just shall live by faith (Hebrew 3:11).

FAITH means without faith it is impossible to please the Lord (Hebrews 11:6).

Hymn: "My Faith Looks Up To Thee"

RISE ABOVE IT WOMEN OF LIGHT

Rise, shine, give God the Glory, soldiers of the Cross, that ye may be blameless and harmless, women of the light, without rebuke, in the midst of a crooked and perverse nation, among whom you shine as lights in the world. We are all the women of light and women of the day: we are not of the night, nor of darkness. For we were formerly in darkness, but now we are lights in the Lord, therefore walk as women of the light. The Lord has commanded us that He has placed us as a light for the Gentiles, that we should bring salvation to all the ends of the earth. We are the light of the world, a city set on a hill that cannot be hidden. Beloved, the nations will come to your light and Kings to the brightness of your rising. For Zion's sake do not hold your peace, and for your sake do not rest, until the righteousness thereof goes forth as brightness, and the salvation thereof as a lamp that burns. Thus let all thine enemies perish, but those who love the Lord are like the rising of the sun in its might.

BLEST. BROKEN. GIVEN.

To request Mother McCoy for speaking
engagements, contact:

Mother Susie N. McCoy
(386) 274-2905
www.theMotherSuperior.com
www.RefugeOrlando.com
MotherSusieMcCoy@aim.com

Biographical Sketch

Mother Susie N. McCoy is a precious woman of God who persistently pursues the power of Pentecost through the purity of Christian love. She was filled with the Holy Ghost at the age of nine in Scotch Plains, NJ, under the Spiritual leadership of the Late Bishop Robert S. and Mother Annie Grayer. Mother McCoy has faithfully served the Church of our Lord Jesus Christ sixty-six years and continues on the battlefield. She currently serves as Director of Women for Region X, President of the Florida Ecclesiastical Diocese Missionary Department, President of the Greater Refuge Memorial Church Missionary Department and Chair of the WL Bonner Scholarship Committee for the International Missionary Department.

Mother McCoy served as Vice President of Education for the International Women's Council (IWC) from 1997 to 2000. She served as President of the IWC from 2000 until 2003. Her first gift to her officers and staff was a scholarship to attend the W. L. Bonner College. On the first Saturday of the month, those in New York attended classes at the Church of Christ Bible Institute. On the second Saturday, those in Detroit attended classes at the Solomon's Temple Bible Institute; and on the third Saturday, those in Florida attended classes at the WL Bonner College in Columbia, South Carolina. Twenty-six people received Mother McCoy's Presidential gift of wisdom! Additionally, Mother McCoy established the *Mother Susie N. McCoy Scholarship,* which covers the cost of tuition and fees for domestic students; *the Mother Dorothy Anderson Scholarship,* which covers the cost of travel, tuition, and fees for international students, and *the Mother Sandra M. Jones Scholarship,* which gives aid to Christian Schools within the Church of our Lord Jesus Christ.

Mother McCoy promotes Christian education and leads by example. She earned the Associate of Science and

Associate of Arts Degrees from Daytona Beach Community College in 1990. At the age of 70, she graduated with Cum Laude honors and as the salutatorian of her class from the W. L. Bonner College with a Bachelor's of Religious Studies, focus in Women's Ministries. At the age of 73, she graduated with a Master's of Science in Theology from Liberty University. At the age of 75, she will earn the terminal degree of EdS (Educational Specialist), yet plans to complete the remaining 30 dissertation hours for the receipt of an EdD (doctorate in education) by the age 77!

She is renown, Apostolic Mother and Teacher. An avid traveler and senior licensed Missionary; she founded a COOLJC in Pullman WA and has spread the Gospel of Jesus Christ throughout the United States, across six continents and the Caribbean Islands. She is the widow of the Late Bishop Ruel B. McCoy of Belize, British Honduras. They remained married thirty-four years prior to his demise in June of 1993. Bishop McCoy pastored churches in Sorrento, Miami, and Orlando, FL and often referred to his faithful companion and remarkable First Lady as "Sugar Babe." Mother McCoy has four children and two daughters-in-love; Marcus (Benona), Luke (Elaine), Dr. Dorcas and Precious; and seven grandchildren, Marcus, Jr., Luke, Jr., Michael, Lukeeshaa, Markeya, Dondre and Kenshawn; all of whom love her dearly and affectionately esteem her as "Mother Superior."

Mother McCoy's advice for longevity is love God, study God's Word, serve God by sharing His love and His Word with others, spend quality time with family, and laugh aloud. Her greatest desire is to bring light to the dark and love to the unloved by lifting up Jesus in such a way that people everywhere would be compelled to yield to Jesus.

CPSIA information can be obtained at www.ICGtesting.com
Printed in the USA
LVOW10s0813210716

497127LV00005B/10/P

9 781618 635280